TAPROOT

Coming Home to Prairie Hill

TAPROOT

Coming Home to Prairie Hill

Martha Leb Molnar

Verdant Books

Rutland, Vermont and San Francisco

First printing

Cover design and book design by Daniela Molnar
Interior illustrations by Daniela Molnar
Cover art "May Mountain" woodcut © 2012 Sabra Field

Editor: Yvonne Daley
Printed in the United States of America by Northshire Press
Manchester, Vermont

Library of Congress Cataloging-in-Publication Data
Molnar, Martha Leb (1949 -)
Taproot: Coming Home to Prairie Hill/Martha Leb Molnar
ISBN #9781499221077

To my mother, who opened
my eyes to nature's spectacle.

And to Ted, my partner
in the grand adventure.

CONTENTS

PROLOGUE

Taproot: A main root, growing almost vertically downward, from which small branch roots spread out. Plants with taproots are difficult to transplant.

It was not a promising first meeting. Atop a rusted cattle gate, a prominent sign threatened that "Trespassers Will Be Shot." The rutted remnants of a road led past hundreds of apple trees in various stages of death and dying. Those still standing had been twisted into tortured shapes by all the pests and diseases known to apple trees in humid New England. The cows and bulls roaming the land had chewed the leaves off the lower limbs while voles and mice had stripped the bark.

Still, the grass was lush, reaching my chest. The wildflowers were as many and as high. We bushwacked to the top of the hill, sending up clouds of sparrows, bobolinks and red-winged blackbirds.

This is what we saw from the rounded hilltop: the Taconic Mountains, all soft shoulders, climbed in rows in the east. Among them, Birdseye Mountain, a massive hump of rock so steep it seemed two-dimensional, brooded directly over us. The eroded southern hills were dotted with small tilted farms. A little white town sat in the valley to the west, where gentle hills gave way to a long, narrow lake. Beyond that, the Adirondacks lined up for a hundred miles in glistening peaks.

Above all hung the entire bowl of the sky, with high clouds streaming toward us. It was a big western sky, an engulfing and throbbing presence, a force that we were to learn alternately bore down with massing weather, then retreated to a high and benevolent immensity.

We looked, turning in slow circles. The breeze brought the odor of animals and tough grass and tough wildflowers. The silence held all the sounds of earth and heaven. Together the smells and the silence might carry all the acid and grit of Manhattan out of my soul.

I sat on the earth's hard bulk and felt slight, a speck on the planet. And it was a good feeling, not of being lost but of being found. Here were unlimited sun and space, under the skyscape I craved, and enough land for solitude and long walks. Here was deliverance from noise and nonsense, from the overbearing presence of the world. The insulation was thin, but real enough, safe enough to offer respite from my rootless history, from generations of persecution culminating in near extermination.

Within two months we were the exhilarated, joyful, terrified owners of 40 acres of a dying hilltop orchard in south-central Vermont.

We put up a cabin and learned to live a primitive, foreign life. Then we built a house, imprinting the place with a deep and lasting stamp of our presence, and our past, and our future dreams. We set in motion the transformation of a Vermont hill, its return to its original self. And we began our own transformation along with the land. Perhaps we too are reverting to what we once might have been and what we are meant to be again.

Pansies

It's too early even for seeds. They'll just sit there, soaking in the cold rain, battling the cold soil. It's certainly too early for geraniums or pansies. In the Northwest I've seen them grow in pots all winter, but early April in Vermont could be winter, a hard New England winter following a string of false spring days.

I plant the pansies anyway. If there's no hard frost, they'll spread, and soon I'll have thriving clumps to fill, then overflow, the large planters by the front door. For now, I put them in individual pots and walk them to the small pines. Under their low branches, they'll sit out the cold like penguin chicks, snug under their fathers' leg feathers until it's time to expose them to the weather.

The pansies look back at me out of their cheerful yellow and lavender faces. Lions mostly. That's what those faces are. After so many decades, pansies continue to hold all the magic they did when I was a child and pansies grew rampant in our city garden in Cluj, an old Transylvanian city in Romania.

We lived on a street lined with chestnut trees. The city's main park, just a short distance away, was an eastern European version of formal French landscape design, with wide boulevards for strolling, dandelions for stringing into necklaces and tiaras, and a lake for boating and ice skating. I loved all these places, tame and safe, with clearly defined borders, which were nevertheless so much more mysterious and thrilling than life inside our house or relatives' houses, where the adults talked and talked about terrible things.

But it was our garden, shady and damp, hidden from the street by a stone fence and overgrown shrubs that offered a daily haven.

Romania in the 1950s was a poor country, squeezed under the Soviet thumb. My father had managed, through bold bribery, to retain his tailoring shop and employ two or three apprentices. We were therefore better off than most. Our house was relatively large and had hot running water. Our pantry was filled with shelves of glossy preserved fruit and we had meat several times a week. On special occasions, I was given chocolates and oranges, imported from exotic places and secured with huge bribes. As only the second child and the first girl born into the remnant of our extended family, I was a symbol of survival and regeneration, and more than that: a miracle, utterly spoiled and endlessly loved.

Still, there was no television, virtually no toys and a meager supply of picture books. I was an only child until age six, and there were very few children among the family members who had survived the Holocaust and those of my parents' social circle. School didn't start until age seven, and my most grand gift, a bicycle, didn't arrive until just a year earlier. So make-believe, by myself, was the entertainment of choice. And it was always better outdoors.

Make believe was inhabited not by the people who actually lived in my world, but by vague historical events and characters from the single book of fairy tales I owned. In my solitary games, vanquishing Turks mingled with tormenting Nazis, and I stranded both in the prickly bushes where their skin was torn to shreds and their eyes consumed by the fantastic insects I gathered or the stinging bees I chased toward them. Sleeping Beauty slumbered in a green cave of overarching shrubs, and princes flew over the treetops. My only live companions were the ants, for whom I built forts made of stones and planted gardens of decapitated flowers. The ants were intransigent, but with the aid of water, shovel and endless time, I managed to sometimes bend their movements to my will.

The pansies were my real friends. Being plants and immobile, they always did my bidding. They had faces, happy ones, with crinkly black eyes and furry lashes, and wide smiling mouths in an upside-down heart shape. Best of all, with their varieties of color and markings, they were all different, like people, and could be turned into any imagined heroine or villain.

The world of the garden was an escape from the adults, who pinched my cheeks, exclaimed over my height, and begged hugs and kisses. The incessant demand that I smile was frightening. As living proof that Hitler had failed, I was expected to be radiantly cheerful, a chubby package of pink cheeks and beribboned laughter. But I was thin, serious and thoughtful, perhaps made so by the emotional husks with whom I lived, whose reliving of the horrors they'd experienced in words and glances, in tormented faces, accompanied every moment.

In the garden, they couldn't see me and I couldn't hear them. Insulated from the adult world and its endless narratives of suffering and death, I was safe in the shrubbery, my head bent to examine a seed head or over the demanding construction of a mud house for the pansy-people. In the garden, I learned how to make the outdoors my refuge, my claim on sanity, igniting a flame of pure and lasting love for the natural world.

When I was six, my mother spent a week in a hospital just outside the city. On Sunday, my father and I went to visit. I remember nothing about the bus ride, the hospital, my mother being ill or any worries I might have had. I also don't remember how I sneaked away, leaving my father holding my mother's hand and their fading voices as I moved away from the open door, then quickly down the long hallway. What I remember clearly is the fascinating world outside as I wandered to the tall trees beyond the cleared area by the building.

Here suddenly was nature on a new scale, vastly larger and more intricate than our little garden or even the city park. The trees didn't follow the straight lines of the chestnuts on our sidewalk or the oaks along the park boulevards. Here, there were no paths to follow at all. I could walk anywhere, my steps muffled on the dark forest floor, hidden from the world.

A messy place, with towering trees whose branches began far above my head, with undergrowth that made walking difficult and getting lost easy. Ferns grew thick at the feet of the giants. I climbed over massive roots, upholstered with blackgreen moss. Dark berries grew in the few open patches. Lost to the world of humans and their fears, I gorged on their winey juiciness. A branch with prongs at its end became a tool for digging under the layers of fallen leaves. There I saw a universe of earthworms and glossy black beetles. Vernal pools glimmered darkly and I stirred each one with muddy hands.

The air shimmered green. I climbed toward a knoll and scrambled to the topmost boulder. I could see an open field, where all was drenched in sun. I walked there and sat down, and the tall grass bent over me, holding me in a feathery nest.

Later, back in the woods, I sat on a log and listened, but heard no familiar sounds. The only reminder of the world was the wind in the treetops, which came from somewhere far away, even more mysterious than this forest. My adored father, my mother sick in the hospital, the loving aunts and uncles, all were remote and unmissed. Alone but not lonely, and utterly unafraid. Thirsty, probably hungry, but unaware of either in this wild, seductive world. I was bewitched.

I must have been gone a very long time because by the time I was found by my father and some strange men, the sun had set. It wasn't until I had children of my own that I thought of what my father had endured the afternoon I discovered wilderness.

The Green Inside Us

When I gave up my position in 2008 and packed up my office to work remotely from Vermont, and gave up title, benefits, the larger chunk of my salary and future advancements, I also gave away everything that had made the space mine over the years. Among the few items I took with me was a photograph that now hangs above my desk. I had cut it out of a magazine long before and had it professionally framed. It shows three weathered buildings: a farmhouse, a barn and an outbuilding. Each is a simple cube with a hipped roof. They stand on a hilltop, alone, a grassy slope in front, a dark sky behind.

Why spend good money framing a cheap magazine photo? Because there was something in that plain composition that I needed to have, if only on a wall. Some vital energy glowed in the simplicity, the openness, the solitude. Its harmony awakened a longing. I loved this place I had never seen, would never see. I already belonged to it.

"Tell me the landscape in which you live and I will tell you who you are," philosopher Joseph Ortega y Gassett wrote. We must be hard-wired for our hearts to open to specific places. For many, that place is by the ocean or among mountains; for just as many, it's likely to be in a city or a suburban street. Someone I know feels perfectly content in New York City's subway system. There must be some bizarre chemistry at work in these bonds, which are often irrational. People who grew up imprinted by wide open spaces regard Manhattan's canyons as home, while others, who, like our children, grew up in leafy suburbs avoid them for a lifetime.

Certainly there was nothing in my upbringing or my family history that would explain my irrational craving to live in a place like the one in the photo. My ancestors were neither farmers nor landed aristocrats. They were – at least for the two or three generations preceding mine, which is as far as my meager knowledge reaches – poor Eastern European Jews who earned their living as cobblers, tailors or, if lucky, as tavern keepers. My grandparents on both sides had ten to twelve children. They were poor by any standard, but my father's family wore shoes and underwear year round. And all of them, every last one, lived in cities or moved to them as soon as they could. Those who lived in villages had no land nor aspired to any; their ambition was to move up in the world, from village to city. A city dweller was superior on every social and economic scale to a country bumpkin.

To my parents, forests and open land held terrors far beyond a drop in social status. Auschwitz was in a remote countryside, adding to my city-bred mother's horror when she struggled out of the cattle car. When she returned, an orphaned cadaver, it was to the city. As a slave laborer, my father had nearly perished on winter marches through the scenic Carpathian Mountains. He survived what his brothers didn't only because his craft as a tailor kept him indoors more. Scenery meant danger. Safety, such as there was, was to be found in cities. It was in the city that my parents were able to live again among other survivors. It was where they met and married and where I was born.

But I, born and raised in a city, craved something else. The colors, the silence, the breadth of that afternoon in the forest lived in the recesses of my mind. I wore it like a hidden souvenir thumping reassuringly against my chest as I walked, and ate, and slept, and later in first grade, when I sat among forty seven-year-olds, more alone than I'd ever been.

Cluj was part of Hungary until after World War I when it was ceded to Romania. At home we spoke Hungarian. So on the first day of school, unable to ask permission to go to the bathroom in Romanian, I gave in to nature, then watched with horror the puddle forming under my chair. It was not an event that was ever forgotten, least of all by my classmates. Eventually, their taunts turned into vague snickering. After a time, I was deaf to both. I was listening to the remembered silence in the tall trees.

My mother was high-strung, with powerful emotions that regularly boiled over. She cried as easily and as often over her own suffering as over everyone else's misfortunes. She cried each time she read me the story of the little matchgirl who froze to death while passersby ignored her. Her sorrows found their way into intricately rhymed poetry, often expansions on poems she composed and memorized in Auschwitz. More often, they ended in rage precipitated by big or small events, exploding in a torrent of screaming. It was never directed at me, although once, overhearing my whining as my hair was being washed, she put her fist through the glass in the bathroom door. Jumping up, the water dripping off my body, I watched the blood drip from her hand, hanging bodiless inside the bathroom. She withdrew it slowly, the catharsis of fury ending in contrite calm. I sat back in the water, my hands remembering, stirring the steaming water.

Five is when our earliest memories are formed. Are everyone's traumatic? Or do others, growing up in cheerful families, have cheerful memories? My daughter Daniela remembers the pink Miss Piggy tricycle with the silver streamers. My son Gabriel remembers his birthday party with shoebox piñatas hung in the trees. His brother David remembers watching a blizzard snap off half the oak in front of our house.

A young aunt who survived Auschwitz as a teenager died of breast cancer when I was five. More than her tragic, painful death, the details of being separated from her little boy in Auschwitz was the subject of hushed, teary talk. What little boy, I wondered? I didn't know any little boys, only my cousin Peter who belonged, I was sure, to a different aunt, and who in any case was not little, being nine years old already. I looked for the little boy, pulling off the white sheets that covered the mirrors after my aunt's death. I was reprimanded, told the sheets must remain for seven days and I must not touch them. I didn't. I moved quietly from window to window in the hush that had descended on my noisy aunts and uncles. I stared at the cement in the courtyard and wished it would turn soft and dark, a rich darkness of many deep shades.

That same year, a little girl moved in a few doors down, then moved out of my life as suddenly as she entered it. We played in the courtyard mostly or along the narrow landings. We slid down the banisters, she following me tentatively, until wearing no stockings one day, she slid down a banister that left her inner thighs filled with splinters She was kept away from me after that for a while. When she was allowed to play with me again, I chose a safe indoor game. Beauty parlor.

It did not end well. Pretending with fingers led to real scissors, and snipping of stray hairs led to wholesale chopping. Not until her long hair lay in mounds at my feet did I start to wonder whether I may have cut just a tad too much. My suspicion was verified in the stricken faces of the adults who found us.

I retreated. Back to the window, to the boulders in the forest, to the wind in the treetops.

Thanks to the greed of Nicolae Ceaușescu, Romania's ruling despot, those first two unhappy school years ended abruptly. My family was allowed to leave the country when Israel paid the per-person ransom. We moved from the old, crumbling city, weekly opera performances and a formal park to a hastily constructed development outside Jerusalem where the weekly entertainment was a jumpy movie in a dusty square, where instead of two languages a dozen were spoken, where everything was new and raw. Not yet a town or even a suburb, our neighborhood was a collection of three-story buildings, their stone facades barely distinguishable from the barren, rock-strewn hills from which they rose, an outpost of the driving need to house the tens of thousands of immigrants arriving in Israel in the '50s and '60s. I took the bus into the city each day, walking to and from school past the prison where Adolph Eichmann was kept in 1961, reliving on each walk the national obsession, compounded by my history, with the first Nazi trial held in Israel.

After school and during the long summers, with parents at work, the children were left to pursue their separate lives, roaming in and out of each other's apartments and congregating under the few trees in "the park."

I learned the new language quickly, and being a child, became acclimated within months. Most of my time was spent with the flocks of children, following the happy discovery that I could not only enjoy the company of peers but could even become popular in a new setting where my pathetic start was unknown. But several times a week I would wander off toward the edge of the settlement where the ground swelled and then flattened out and the emptiness began.

Here a sparse Mediterranean forest stretched for some three miles, all the way to the Hebrew University. It was a wild place, radically unlike the landscaped park in Cluj or even the forested hospital grounds. It was marked by thousands of years of history, but this was unknown to me. A sculpture park of fantastically shaped limestone rocks, carved and deeply pitted, paeans to the power of water and wind. Open to the sky, its few large trees – stocky Tabor oaks, tall carob, eucalyptus and Aleppo pines, twisted, hoary relics – had miraculously been saved from the saw that had over the centuries decimated the Biblical cedars and most other trees. Dry tan grass and prickly pear cactus that yielded no fruit grew between the widely spaced trees and boulders. Snakes and scorpions lived here, but more frightening were the mines that remained from the 1948 War of Independence. A boy from our building was killed one summer day when he stepped on one.

The place was mine. I never met another person there, child or adult. I went there in every season, because each offered gifts. Spring arrived in February after the winter rains. The grass turned a vibrant green, the cactus flowered brilliantly and from every pocket in the rocks flaming orange anemones and pale pink cyclamen burst forth. I gathered armfuls of these to bring home, clambering over boulders, stepping where I couldn't see the snakes sunning, wandering great distances. In summer, when the burning dry *hamsin* winds blew from the Jordanian desert, when people stayed indoors with the windows closed and the stone floors kept damp, I sat under the meager greenness of the oaks and pines. Forced by the heat to sit rather than roam, there was time to observe the differing leaves and feel the trunks, to bury acorns in rock soil, to watch the shimmer of heat in the near distance and the arc of the sun across the flat blue sky. Fall, not clearly a season in that climate, was simply a pleasanter summer when I could comfortably walk all the way to the university and back, kicking stones and examining a universe of fallen fruit, seeds, husks, none edible but intriguing in their variety. Only wet winter days kept me away; I have never felt anything but intense dislike to being rained on.

I was happy in my wanderings. Then, another move, and my world was again radically altered.

I was 13 when we moved to New York City. My American aunt had visited us, and seeing my mother haul ice for the icebox, the upright crate that served as our wardrobe, and my brother and me sleeping on the floor so an unemployed uncle and his wife could sleep in beds, suggested we move to America, "at least for a few years." Seduced by rosy depictions of life in America, my parents began the immigration process.

We arrived in early February, after two bitter weeks at sea in the bowels of the ship. The first sight of Manhattan's skyline was a thrill. I couldn't know how much I would be losing, that I wouldn't see long views and open sky until my first trip to the American West a decade later.

The South Bronx in the winter of 1963 was as far from the flowering hills of Jerusalem as one could go and still remain on the same planet. Dirty snow piled waist high on the frigid streets, streets that remained gray in the sunshine that came with the late spring. Color and softness had no place in this world of stained brick where trash was incinerated and coal burned and the chimneys spewed all day and night. The marigolds I planted on the fire escape and the caged bird in the house died in the murky, dank air. The marigolds, I realized, could survive without regular watering but needed sun. The bird could live without sun but needed regular feeding. The deaths were not surprising and barely sad. They confirmed what I already knew: this was a place where no life – the marigolds', the bird's or mine – could flourish.

School was one of two places where life felt energized. My father bought the *New York Daily News* the first day he went to work, and read it on the subway ride to the factory in Brooklyn. He was determined to learn English, as much for practical reasons as so he could stop speaking Hungarian. It was, he said, the language of anti-Semites, of the mobs who turned the Danube red with Jewish blood.

While he read the newspaper, I read and reread the *Anne of Green Gables* books. Since I already knew the stories from having read them in Hebrew, it was easy to guess at the meanings of words and phrases. Within six months I understood everything and could speak a serviceable English. And aside from *Romeo and Juliet,* I managed the 8th grade well enough that the teachers took notice. Even the administration took notice when the shocking discrepancy between the IQ test, administered three months after we arrived, and the reading test, administered six months later, became evident. I was far below borderline on the first, and well beyond eighth grade on the second. My parents were called. My mother arrived at the appointed time, at approximately the same minute that John F. Kennedy was assassinated. With her English limited to a few phrases, she didn't clearly understand what had happened until that evening, when my aunt and cousins called to explain. I understood the event but being thirteen and new to the country, nothing of its import. In any case, the meeting with the teacher was skipped and the mystery of my test scores was ignored. I continued reading voraciously. But it would take another and a different life to make me appreciate the Bard.

The other outlet was my aunt's house, some forty miles north of the ashen, rapidly declining Bronx. A farmhouse built in what used to be a potato field, it had a broad, soggy lawn surrounded by a fringe of forest and noxious swamps (this was before they became cherished wetlands) that was central address for a vast population of unnaturally large and lively mosquitoes. It also had a productive vegetable garden, blackberries, raspberries and green gooseberries, massive dahlias, and a huge oak that shaded the crumbling patio. And there was sun that sometimes shone all day, unimpeded by hundreds of blocks of dingy buildings, and air, pure compared to the coal dust blowing in the Bronx. I learned to plant beans, shell peas by the hour, weed roses. I learned that one could spend entire days outdoors, being happily productive. That life was better lived by the rising and setting of the sun.

Three years after our arrival, my parents bought a small row house in Queens, a minor economic miracle. Both worked at low-wage jobs in textile factories, taking the subway from the Bronx to Brooklyn and returning late, spent. Evenings, the four of us threaded needles with rough black thread to speed my mother's piecework the next day. I was thirteen, old enough to go directly after school to babysit two small children while their impoverished single mother worked. I resented spending what could have been reading time with those whining, snotty children. I made sure they were safe, but provided little affection. Many years later, when I had children of my own, I thought often about those children guiltily and felt grateful that I got to mostly raise my children myself.

My parents loved that tiny house every day of the forty-five years they lived there. The morning sun lit the two bedrooms while the afternoon sun brightened the living room and miniscule kitchen. The street trees and the stamp-sized front yard were a gift. A young scarlet oak had already overgrown one side of the yard, a couple of my mother's beloved hot pink azaleas and a climbing rose filled the other.

My father insisted on a lawn, by necessity no larger than a throw rug. He was a thoroughly urban creature who knew nothing about plants nor cared about them beyond their value in raising our modest house to barely bourgeois. To the end of his life just weeks before his 99th birthday, he remained baffled by my desire to live in "vilderness," where "you see trees, just like you see them here. Why you need so many trees? One, two, three, enough, like children. Too many, too much trouble, you don't see the people from the trees." People were interesting, and they mattered. People determined life and death, not trees.

But the lawn was a symbol of the American dream. So he threw great quantities of seeds on the hard clay and drowned them daily, then watched the spindly grass come up with great satisfaction. The real reward was when, still looking like a comb-over, the grass got tall enough to need trimming. Then he brought out his large tailoring shears and ceremoniously trimmed each blade to a height best suited to a large golf course. He insisted on pruning the azaleas too, to what he deemed a neat and elegant size. My mother, on the other hand, firmly believed the azaleas should be allowed to grow to the roof if they so chose and forbade him to touch them. But being a tailor used to fitting fabric to life, he found the wildly reaching shoots intolerable and resorted to subterfuge, which he then attempted to deny in the face of incontrovertible and terrible results. The azaleas became the source of a war between my parents that flared up every spring and lasted until the last six months of my mother's life, when she became too disoriented to notice the murderous damage.

I, on the other hand, soon lost interest in our tiny yard. The trees on the sidewalk provided only the illusion of a barrier to the traffic speeding down the wide street and the city bus that stopped in front of the house. People would stop to chat. Neighbors, strangers, bus drivers. Whether weeding or hiding behind the maple, I had unwanted company. The yard was simply too small to meet the most downsized requirements.

Once I discovered Flushing Meadow Park, site of the 1963 World's Fair, I never sat on the porch again.

The park consisted of a muddy, man-made lake surrounded by willows. Highways, including the notorious Long Island Expressway, ringed it on every side. But sitting under the weeping willows and facing the lake, I could shut out the traffic, the planes that swooped low as they neared the two airports, and the cigarette butts in the grass -- especially when reading. Which is what I did most weekdays after sneaking out of the large city high school, where the absence of one quiet girl was never noted. In effect, I missed most of high school, passing the state regents exams and performing creditably on the SATs through cramming and memorizing. I learned no history or science, and math remained a mystery. To this day, the memory of those recurring questions about two trains traveling at different velocities and arriving at the same time to a converging point chills my very organs.

Amaryllis

The news is bleak. The world's famines and wars, its sheer evil persists alongside its beneficence and beauty. There is beauty in the bent necks of the horses in the neighbor's pasture, in the denuded hedgerow even, and in the dry amaryllis and paperwhite bulbs I'm placing in a pot. I am filling the pots halfway with soil, positioning the flower bulbs, then fitting more soil around, drizzling in warm water that percolates to the roots and emerges in a dark streak at the bottom of the pots.

The horses line themselves up in parallel rows, leaving equidistant gaps from each other, their heads to the ground, silently chewing on whatever they find in the frozen earth. Why do they line themselves up this way? It seemed mysterious, until I read that they stand in each other's wind shadow.

They're a study in still life, a portrait in black, white and brown against the gray landscape. From where does such patience come? Such resignation? No response came yesterday when I walked to the fence and spoke to them. Perhaps it's plain animal dumbness. Perhaps it's something else, an equine arrogance, a refusal to squander their energy on the little the world offers beyond food. Better to mind the bleached grass sticking through the cold earth.

The Adirondacks are a panorama of snowy pyramids in the kitchen window. They bolt out against the flat blue sky. There are nine of them, carefully counted and named by me. There are the Three Sisters in the center of the range, flanked by Adi, Ron and Dack on the right. On the left, in descending order, Venti, Grande and Tall. They too hunker there, cold and indifferent. One day I will search them out and find the way to their summits. I need to not just lift mine eyes onto the hills, but haul myself up them too. Then, having put time and effort into finding them, and sweat and fear into climbing them, and having measured my slightness against their bulk, they will be mine despite their distance and indifference.

The paperwhites or the crimson amaryllis? Which will look best against the window that will soon frame a landscape of snow? Will it be the peaceful uniformity of white against white, an amalgam of every color on earth and of no color? Or the stark contrast of red heat against cold? My fingers descend into the warm earth in the pots, and push the dry bulbs further in, so hard with life and promise. I am content. The sheer luxury of doing just one thing at a time! But then I stop guiltily. Do I have a right to this? Is it proper to be almost vibrating with silent joy at the pleasure of this hour, an hour when natural and man-made disasters, tsunamis and wars, droughts and terror, mud slides and hunger and infected water are laying waste to millions?

I have no say in the matter. It's not up to me at all. I came to this place and now it's telling me how to live.

On Uphill Road

The real estate agent, a genteel late middle-aged man impeccably dressed for golfing, had shown us six properties on our first foray for land, some with houses, some without. They were all ten acres, except for the two that were six acres. This was ten times our current acre, a tenfold increase in our holdings and as a logical sequel, our concomitant happiness. Instead, we were immediately confronted with this surprising fact: we knew, with full certainty, that these properties would not make us happy. Despite their relative hugeness, they seemed narrow, confining, dull. Later, when we heard them referred to as "spaghetti" lots, we understood why.

The realtor noticed our fallen faces after the first two showings.

"We'll look at just a couple more, but only for comparison purposes," he assured us. So he could better understand our "vision." On the way to the last four, we went into great detail describing our vision.

"Ten acres seems like enough but maybe we need more after all," Ted said.

"We want a varied landscape, not all woods," I added. "We sort of live in the woods now, so we really want long views, and maybe a pond or a river."

"We need complete privacy."

"And we don't want to be in the mountains."

"Four extra weeks of winter? Definitely not for us."

"But it should have some ups and downs, otherwise it's dull."

"But not steep, just gentle rises."

The list continued while the realtor listened, nodding gravely.

When he left us at the end of the day, he gently suggested that we consider areas further north, perhaps much further north. He never called again.

Disappointed but undaunted, we found another realtor and headed back to Vermont from New York the following weekend. In the warming air, we were bursting with renewed hope and good cheer. This new realtor showed us parcels that "with a little bit of imagination" and the cutting of many acres of trees, would yield a narrow view, sort of like looking through a camera lens. Finally, we were shown one hundred acres encompassing a hilltop and stretching up a steep slope. We loved it immediately, and ignored the expense of putting in an outrageously long driveway and electric lines the same length. The real issue was that it was listed for 150 percent above our budget.

But the charming realtor, whom we liked immediately, assured us he really liked us too, and more importantly, understood what we wanted and why we wanted it. He himself, when he came to Vermont back in the '70s as a back-to-the-lander, had the same dream. He promised that he "will not rest" until he finds the land meant for us, because we "absolutely, definitely, incontrovertibly" deserve it. We could only nod and smile widely.

"And why the hell not?" he asked. This was his favorite rhetorical question, and very effective in its ability to inspire confidence, no matter how oft repeated. Long views? Well, why the hell not? Total privacy? Sure, why the hell not? Open fields? Can't see why the hell not!

Problem was, despite the mutual admiration-fest, this very special realtor had many special passions of his own. His beloved miniature evergreens, his musical performances and his many good friends' musical performances, which ranged throughout the year on most weekends, began to seriously interfere with our search. After his third weekend off in a row, we understood that his generous embrace of our passion would never result in any progress.

We fired him. He wished us luck.

We were what realtors call "highly motivated buyers." So why did they seem less interested in us than we in them? Why were they not competing for our certain buy? True, our purchase would not yield a major increase in their income, but we were two birds in the hand, right? Was there something about Vermonters that made them less interested in making money than people elsewhere, especially New York where making money was, after all, the main point?

A new real estate agent came highly recommended by a mutual friend. I reviewed our disappointing history and laid out our unchanged list of requirements. She listened sympathetically, nodding in agreement, although professional discretion prevented her from excoriating other agents as I was sure she wanted to. She promised to do thorough research and contact us very soon. She never did.

Deep inside us is a quest for home, a vision formed when we were children. When we meet it later in life, we know we are home. Conceived in the fog of childhood, kept dormant through decades of breathless, busy days, my vision reached weak tendrils toward the light of recognition when it finally had a chance to flourish. And flourish it did, finding a voice, painting a vision that rapidly became fact. All it needed was the canvas. That canvas was land.

There is nothing more real than land. The search for it was like the search for a mate, for love, sustenance, partnership and amusement. I was prepared to offer love and loyalty and care in return.

I knew a great deal about love relationships, having been married since just before I turned twenty and having had three children before I reached thirty. And I knew that I had a mate who shared some of my vision.

I met my future husband in the first month of my last year in high school in 1967. Ted was tall and handsome, with blue eyes and thick curly hair. A year and a half older than me, he was worldly and sophisticated. His background was almost identical to mine, except he was born in Hungary instead of the formerly Hungarian part of Romania. Like me, his family left Hungary for Israel when he was ten, and after several years, when he was a teenager, moved to Queens to join other family members. Ted was already in his first year of college, an aspect I found impressive. Most important, he shared my passion for the outdoors.

After landing a well-paying summer job at the Fulton Fish Market with the added perk of free fish, which he carried home on the crowded subway, creating regal personal space, Ted managed to scrape together enough to buy a 1950 Pontiac that usually started up and had working windows. That huge, ungainly car became our ticket to the green world beyond stifling Queens. Most weekends we'd drive over the bridge, heading north to where the trees outnumbered the houses, and then to where the houses dwindled until we saw only trees. A large state park was our usual destination, where we could quickly leave the crowds barbecuing by the lakefront and head into the woods. We hiked the low hills, searching for the most scenic point to unwrap the thick sandwiches of mayonnaise and cheese, losing and finding our way, arriving miles from the car, hitching rides in the failing light. On every such day I was restored to a self that was joyful and full of wonder.

But as always, the day shriveled to the unforgiving drive back to Queens, the arching brown smudge on the horizon closing in, the crowded skyline a terrible affront to our forest-saturated eyes.

We married in my senior year in college. When my daughter was the same age, I realized that we had not been merely young; we had been barely adults. The fact that we were invincible in our conviction that we knew what we were doing was living proof that we still had one leg in childhood. With the arrival of three children, financial pressures and family tragedies, we rapidly lost that unfounded belief in our fundamental rightness. We were changing, profoundly, but had no time to notice.

Before our youngest, Daniela, was born in 1979, just nineteen months after her brother Gabriel and six years after David, we left our tiny row house in Queens for the suburbs, or the exurbs that northern Westchester was then. We bought a roomy high-ranch, a most prosaic wooden rectangle, the defining hallmark of the deadly 1960s tract developments.

Its attraction lay precisely in the fact that it wasn't in a development. It was at the confluence of three narrow winding wooded roads dating to Revolutionary times. The houses, mostly summer cottages built in the '20s and expanded into year-round homes, were widely spaced. Best, behind the house were acres of undeveloped land, of which one whole acre was ours, making us feel like landed gentry. Some two-thirds of the acre was in lawn, the rest woodland that mingled into the hundred acres of woods that belonged to others, but being empty and bordering on our back yard, it all felt like ours. Once farmed land, we were charmed to discover in these woods ancient apple trees, a network of crumbling stone walls, and an array of rusted farm machinery that our children preferred over the jungle gym we installed, and which they miraculously survived to reach adulthood.

We lived in that house for twenty-nine years. A part-time college instructor and full-time mother for a decade, I set out to forge a new career when our youngest started first grade, carving a meandering path from reporter for a regional newspaper, to freelance writer for *The New York Times,* finally landing in public relations, an option that offered a wage beyond the babysitter costs. Ted, meanwhile, valiantly devoted himself to almost single-handedly supporting five people, spending his days in one office or another, battling his screaming need for physical movement and the outdoors, returning from a long commute in time for a hurried dinner and most nights, to more hours devoted to an importing business he was trying to build in a corner of the basement he shared with the trampoline.

I managed our finances so that we were free of debt. We were often down to one car, with Ted walking a mile to the bus to the train. Summers we rented a cottage somewhere in New England for a week, always near a lake or the ocean. I cooked everything from scratch and we ate out only if I was reviewing a restaurant for the paper, in which case everyone got to pick three full courses from the menu with no limits set. Our children were nearly teenagers before they flew on a plane, having convinced us that they were the only children in the town, in the county, in the whole New York Metro area and possibly in the entire country, who had not been to Disney World.

Grateful for the luxury of being a mostly stay-at-home mother and helplessly in love with my children, I was nevertheless often overcome by the emotional demands of raising them. Personal time was rare, and solitude nonexistent. A journal I kept sporadically during those years, an attempt to solve the puzzle of being so busy and accomplishing so little, reports an endless catalogue of tasks and even more gaps, presumably filled with such unrecorded events as washing scraped knees, comforting one or another crying child, diaper changing and toilet training, washing up spilt food or blood, dressing children in snowsuits and immediately undressing them for a bathroom call, searching for lost hats, mittens and toys, and buckling rebellious kids into car seats.

They were difficult years, with frustration erupting in contrasting ways, the dark lava cooling into accumulating ash that sometimes threatened to bury us. I joked that what I needed most was a wife, a stay-at-home one who would make the kind of home I was striving to create. A home filled with the aroma of baking bread and apple pie, of spotless floors and organized toys. Plus a thriving garden to provide healthy greens for every meal and cut flowers for every room. And most importantly, a wife with endless patience for three children and a stressed-out husband.

Despite what, looking back now, seems like superhuman energy, neither my mothering nor my marriage, nor my home nor my garden ever lived up to those ideals. Still, our careers progressed, changed, evolved. Well into November, wearing parkas under their bibs, the children learned to eat all their meals on the deck and to look for amusement and joy in the woods. They grew strong and were rarely sick. They passed through their teens with just garden-variety angst, and grew into good people and accomplished adults, people I would want as my friends if they weren't my children.

After all the years of shaping our lives around them, they each left, as we'd hoped they would. Having had to always consider our parents' emotional wellbeing before considering our own – a common trait among children of survivors – we taught our children to not feel responsible for our happiness. They learned the lesson extremely well, each pursuing his or her adventures, leaving me spending nights in cold terror at the endless possibilities for illness, accidents, attacks, death. Eventually, each found a niche and a partner, and they moved out for good.

We were left with the proverbial empty nest, a condition I had at times desperately craved. And I was suddenly bereft. For a couple of years I continued to shop and cook for a family, to mail their favorite foods in special packaging, to wish I hadn't allowed them to go to colleges so far away. Then, still missing them, I decided I liked my new, relatively carefree life.

As the pressures eased, we had time to notice that we too had been drastically altered by time and by each other. We began to assess our lives. Everything was evaluated: my daily commute and once-loved job, Ted's increasingly onerous, lonely work on his home-based business, the house and neighborhood, the friends we liked and those we didn't, even the climate. Under this intense examination, we found that many things no longer fit. We had no answers yet, only mounting questions.

Owls

Later, after we had found some answers and were living on our hill, the big and small questions persisted. Such as the one about the owl and the pussycat.

A great horned owl, perched on the barn roof. Its magnificent bulk was visible from a distance. We saw it circle the hill on heavy owl wings, slide silently over the fields, its bent talons and hooked beak pointing at us. Sometimes it rose to one of three ash trees and landed heavily, bending the branches and wavering for minutes, seemingly enjoying swinging in the air.

Where it roosted was a mystery. Not anywhere near the barn. It used the roof as a convenient perch, that's all. Even when still, displaying its pale belly to our probing eyes, it guarded its secrets. Its wildness was in the tiger stripes in its plumage, its golden ear tufts, its cold yellow iris, its deadly talons.

By early winter, the owl was dead. I found its feathers strewn on the frozen ground by an apple tree. From the small handful, I knew without doubt that they belonged to the owl. I knew its neck had been snapped and it had been left to rot where I couldn't find it.

Was it the feral cat, that large pale animal streaking through the fields? Was it the large dog from the house at the end of the road that visited us occasionally? Maybe a raccoon or fox. Or maybe the owl was old, ill, and its time had come to die and feed others.

All the rest of that year, its missing bulk hovered in the edges of the twilight. It came to us from an unknown place, lent its beauty to the air, and vanished, taking its special wildness from us. Other owls had come and quickly gone, but none has taken its place.

A snowy owl visited us another late fall. It too perched on the barn roof. I saw it while walking down to the mailbox one afternoon. I saw it but was sure I was wrong. Snowy owls, as far as I knew, aren't seen in Vermont. So I returned with binoculars and stared at it. I walked closer and closer, the dead grass under a dusting of powdery snow making no sound. It saw me of course; it can see the movement of a mouse under snow. But I thought if I walked very slowly and silently I might blend into the landscape, no greater a threat than a tree blowing in the wind.

The owl stared dead ahead. Regal in its calm, it blended into the white stillness. It brought with it the vast emptiness of the tundra. Staring at the bird, which never bothered to return my stare, I felt a great chill. But what was this owl doing here anyway? And why was it out in broad daylight?

Every so often there are, it turns out, southward irruptions of birds from the far north, driven by the same forces that drive our lives: food and sex. During years when the lemming population is high – their main food source – owls and other Arctic raptors have more prey to feed their young, increasing their population. Success is followed by hunger, because more owls need more lemmings. The young are forced to migrate into southern Canada and further south, right into our tiny dot of Vermont , avoiding competition with the more aggressive adult birds. And since daylight in the Arctic summer reigns for nearly twenty-four hours, they adapt to hunting any time.

Our open white fields must have felt like home to this visitor. But within days it too was gone. I never found its feathers. I believe the owl and cat never saw each other.

That cat. Troubles with the cat didn't begin or end with the owl. I regularly meet its slinking form in the fields. Its intent is clear. House cats – feral or winningly domesticated – are a scourge on birds, killing millions of them each year. "Scientists estimate that free-roaming cats kill hundreds of millions of birds, small mammals, reptiles and amphibians each year," the Virginia-based American Bird Conservancy, which runs a "Cats Indoors!" campaign, warns on its website. I have no doubt "our" prowling cat kills its weight in birds weekly, the very birds we are dedicated to saving.

The solution was obvious. Remove the cat from our property and take it to some distant place. Let him earn his living by the sweat of his whiskers somewhere else. Someone, town animal warden most obviously, should be able to do that. The warden said yes, he could remove the cat. No problem. How, I inquired. He's so elusive. With a trap, he explained, in a voice reserved for children and idiots. And then? And then what? And then what will he do with the cat? I could have it, he said. But I don't want it, that's the point, isn't it? Well, then, he'd remove the cat. And then what? Then the cat wouldn't catch any more birds, he noted, after a long pause in which he was likely assessing whether my intelligence was anywhere near normal.

I couldn't do that. Who am I to decide who shall live and who shall die? The cat is not a coddled house cat that snaps off birds' heads for sport. It's a clever animal, a hunter that hunts to eat. Is one cat less worthy of life than a dozen birds? Yes, my gut says. And still, it won't allow me to have the cat trapped and killed.

And so each spring when the birds return, I hope the cat had died a natural death.

Homecoming

After twenty-nine years, there was grief in locking the door on our old home for the last time, even though its life force, at least our particular form of life energy, had been gone for some time. In truth, for years before then, the house, the lawn, even the old oaks, had begun to feel amiss.

There was too little room and sun for my expanding gardens. Starting with conventional beds of impatiens and petunias, I slowly graduated to a perennial garden that over time encompassed one whole side of the property and continued around the boulders that dropped to the driveway.

Unplanned, riddled with landscaping errors, this profusion of blooms provided pleasure to the neighborhood. The dog walkers and joggers, bikers and strollers were greeted with an ever-changing palette.

One day, Gabriel's friends stood arrested by the garden, a group of gawky teenage boys hiding their admiration with a loud debate on the excruciating consequences of ingesting the poisonous digitalis. Another time, two burly exterminators who came to rid the house of carpenter ants stopped for minutes by the white Asiatic lilies. Once the neighborhood scrooge, who had barely nodded his head in greeting whenever our paths crossed previously, inquired about the hot pink blooms topping the gray stalks. "Campion," I answered. "Old and invasive, but I like them." I thought this might start an exchange, but he only mumbled as he moved on, "Hadn't seen them since I was a kid. My mother had them all over the place."

The garden was always under threat, because despite decades of effort cultivating that little piece of earth, it was the forest that triumphed. Each year, through droughts, floods and caterpillar attacks, the oaks on the lawn grew visibly mightier. Beyond the lawn, the forest was a tangled, impenetrable web of giants, a solid wall of green that threatened to cross the vernal stream that separated it from the struggling grass and engulf us. The forest, I was convinced, had already sent out invading pioneers, and enormous roots were wrapping themselves around the foundations, sending long slender fingers to poke below the windows. Then spreading branches would crumble the walls, and sodden earth needled with blackberries would obliterate our attempt to invade the forest. I loved the forest and feared its girdling power. I craved light and air free of snagging branches.

The neighbors were also changing. Our narrow road was noticeably busier each year, as soccer moms drove back and forth and hired various services, so that every season was defined by large machines that chopped up the quiet air with buzzing, sawing, chipping, mowing clamor. And while no one else seemed to notice, I was suddenly acutely aware of the Taconic State Parkway, some four miles away, that on quiet mornings seemed to have been moved just behind the woods. Ted, who worked out of the house and therefore spent much more time at home, also felt alienated. The new neighbors were not neighborly, the lines in the post office grew longer, the Colonial–era roads were empty of walkers, loud with SUVs.

The deciding factor came at the annual progressive holiday party. A much-loved neighborhood institution for fifty years in which we walked from house to house for the three-course meal, it was now held at a restaurant. None of the people in the new McMansions that were built on the little land still available wanted to accommodate a large group in their huge homes. I was munching on a stuffed mushroom and trying to balance my glass of wine, chatting amiably with a group of newer, thirty-somethings about the wonderful walking afforded by our winding wooded roads, thinking at the same time about how these people never walked the roads. But it turned out that at least one of them had. Not only walked past our house but apparently walked at least partly down our driveway too. I learned this when she mentioned, very politely, that hanging laundry in my backyard was an eyesore. She didn't use that word of course. "Not appropriate" was what I think she said.

"But nobody walking from any direction can see it," I protested. "You'd have to literally walk onto our property to see it!"

Nevertheless, it had been seen, presumably by the only neighbor close enough, and later verified by the lone walker who now smiled warmly while informing me that it was "not in keeping with the area."

I excused myself to refresh my drink and spent the rest of the evening reminiscing with a couple of people I'd known and liked for decades, who were retiring and moving before the next progressive party.

I continued drying the laundry outdoors, taking great satisfaction in using the sun instead of fossil fuels. But we did not attend the following year's progressive party.

I needed out. Out of the house and neighborhood, out of the daily commute, even out of the job I had loved. It was, as I often remarked, the best but last job I'd ever have. As head of the communications department at a successful non-profit that raised funds for the Technion-Israel Institute of Technology in Haifa, a highly regarded university known as Israel's MIT, I had the best of multiple worlds: the intellectual challenge of working with world-class scientists; the satisfaction in being part of the American Jewish community and of being connected to Israel and its achievements; the pleasure of excellent colleagues and close relationships with highly successful donors; and the knowledge that I was in a small, peripheral way contributing to helping people worldwide. Having spent the previous eight years at Readers Digest, where ignoring the often right-wing slant of the magazine articles I publicized was a job requirement, the Technion Society offered deeply satisfying work. And still, I was no longer happy. What should have been a continuum of work, life and play had disintegrated into rigid opposites. I was exhausted from nights spent in wakeful sleep, stressed by the mere knowledge that the morning would bring another day of commuting and relentless activity, *apart* rather than *a part* of life as I began to define it. The definition, somewhat vague, called for a life spent outdoors instead of in meetings, of living by the sun instead of train schedules, of working with hands and body and not just brain. More and more, I felt myself pacing a cage constructed of the "normal" life while longing for freedom.

I was drained of the ambition that once coursed through me, driving me to sleep less, do more, more, more. I lost the desire to move quickly in the world, to rack up achievements. I still felt young, fit, but perhaps the gravity I wasn't feeling was nevertheless claiming its due. I was possessed by a different kind of drive. "Start a huge, foolish project, like Noah," wrote Rumi. For that, I had plenty of energy.

Ted, who hates change, now also craved it. He wanted an adventure, and was flexible about the specifics. Travel, exotic and long, would suffice, he said.

I was not to be mollified by travel. Travel seemed a distraction from building an anchored life with daily novelty and sustenance.

We talked. We talked at dinner and over morning coffee. Ted talked about the narrowing window of time to talk and plan and, finally, do.

"We have ten good years left," he pronounced. "Maybe." This truth became starkly clear at a relative's funeral. Returning to the empty house, the family and friends quickly separated into two distinct groups. There were the children, some of whom were young adults in college or beyond. And there *we* were, the next to go.

There was not enough time to spend five days of every week in Manhattan, where the frenetic pace was turning me into a harridan with a foul mouth, ready to take on every driver inching toward me through *my* green light and every commuter with a loud phone voice. I needed to leave the formal life of schedules and crowds, to wander out of the hedged garden into an unkempt meadow, to create a life with silence at the center of it, a vast silence surrounded by volumes of empty air. I needed to connect to my younger, wilder self, the one that forged our love on the woodland trails in the Hudson Highlands.

Ted listened and understood but his ideas were more amorphous. Less time staring at the computer screen. Learning new skills. He mentioned woodworking, history, baking… and other soon forgotten pursuits. And a smaller house.

"The house is not too big," I argued. "It's laid out all wrong for the two of us."

I pointed out the too many bedrooms, the too small living room, the unused basement.

"It's too big," he insisted.

"It's not too big," I insisted. "It's empty."

We stopped discussing the house and focused on location.

"Why not Colorado?" he asked. Gabriel lived there and the skiing is superb.

I argued that Gabriel was too young to make a permanent home, and if he moved, we'd be left with just mountains.

"Those are not 'just' mountains…" he'd start, extolling the endless months of powder skiing.

"We need to live where we can live the way we want to live," I said after one such conversation.

"We can do that right here," he answered. "In a smaller house."

We couldn't. Or I couldn't. I needed a new life in a place big enough, open enough, private enough to encompass all the old and new cravings, and future dreams too. The concept of a big piece of green and silent land began to grow, its taproot embedding itself in my brain. It grew and strengthened, spreading out multiple stems until I forgot that this was a buried childhood dream recently brought to light of day. I began to believe that it was the only logical direction for my life.

We met with a financial planner. We learned, to our astonishment, that although we continued to live modestly and save wherever we could, we were no longer poor; that we had over the years, as our income increased while our expenses had not, moved up several economic rungs. That our house, being in an old, established area that retained its woodsy charm, was worth more than we imagined. That spending almost nothing on the luxuries others valued -- clothes, cars, restaurants – had paid off. That opting for "experiences" over "things," our standard response to the children's requests for pricier cars and haircuts, promised to soon make us almost economically independent. If we worked and saved for a few more years, we could live on part-time work.

This new finding made Ted very happy. It made me happy too, but more than anything, it strengthened my determination. Ted remained on the fence. Having no alternate plan, he agreed to join me on the adventure, which was at this point nebulous enough to allow for any number of directions that he could accept. There was no harm in looking, he agreed. He didn't yet understand that I had already abandoned the familiar shores and was swimming toward a new destination.

But where?

We culled through memories: On a backpacking trip in Washington State, we had nearly jumped on a forty-acre piece in the high desert with distant views of the Cascades. But when we got home, I worried that I was ignorant about the plants and trees that grew there and couldn't even find the place on a map. We were also made nervous by a metal warehouse filled with canned, freeze-dried, powdered, bottled, bagged provisions transported there by the millenialist owners, who, disappointed that the world persisted beyond 2000, were selling the land. Were they and their ilk populating the remote valley?

I had fallen in love with a tiny island in a Maine lake during another vacation. It held three primitive cabins reached with a leaky rowboat and was restricted by zoning laws that made building a house unlikely. Still, for six whole months I saw a family compound and generations of children screaming with delight in the frigid waters.

A recent ski vacation in Montana offered novel possibilities. The land was being divided into "ranchettes," enormous to me even with their diminutive appellation. But the airport in Bozeman was too close and the whine of trailer trucks carried to the most distant ranchette in the barren landscape.

Nova Scotia and Cape Breton were both beautiful and affordable, and probably warmer than much of New England thanks to the Gulf Stream. But these places were, after all, in another country. We were not willing to ever become foreigners again.

The Rockies were breath stopping in their majesty. And that was precisely the problem. They were too high, too jagged, too austere to ever feel like home. The valleys were either too narrow and claustrophobic or too enormous for my mind to encompass.

Several springs in a row we had visited friends in the California desert. I was struck by how clean the desert was, in a way the overgrown rank Northeast can never be. Each creosote shrub and barrel cactus grew in its own separate realm. One could walk among them as in a carefully maintained garden. And that dry heat, that inferno of drowning light, followed by cool nights and black, star studded skies! It was tempting, despite being foreign. We thought about New Mexico, Arizona.

In the end, they were all too far from our family and friends. I was ready to make a break from a life, not from the people in it.

By this time, the land had become more than the fulfillment of a fantasy. It was to be a haven for our children and their children. It had to have water and soil and climate to grow food. It had to be large enough to allow for several possible future houses for what we hoped would become an extended family. The vision had expanded into nothing less than our collective destiny.

So where was home?

Much closer, it turned out, than the Rockies, the Sonoran Desert or the North Atlantic islands. Less than half a day's drive from New York City. And with plants, animals and climate I understood. Not exotic, not distant. Familiar and perfect.

We had learned to love Vermont in winter from ski trips. But incredibly, we had never seen it in spring or summer or fall. And when we did finally see it for the first time in summer, we understood, with the sudden clarity of obvious truth: here was home.

The intense greenness. The ancient, worn mountains, accessible, inviting. The variegated canopy of green from their peaks, down their rounded slopes, reaching fingers into the lowlands, following the rivers on their westward journeys. The wide valleys with long views of the Green Mountains in the east and New York's Adirondacks in the west. The upland pastures dotted with the quintessential black and white cows and red barns, so storybook perfect they might have been one-dimensional Hollywood props. Later, we learned the pastures and lowland farms were part of Vermont's "working landscape," a patchwork of farms, forests and compact villages. A concept central to the state's economy, its distinctive "brand," and its magnetism to tourists.

Vermont is the second most rural state in the nation, right after Wyoming. But whereas farms in much of the country tend to be industrial sized, Vermont's are tiny by comparison. A hundred acres of grass and corn, along with an acre of vegetables and a small orchard, flanked by forests and a small village are a beautiful sight; a couple of thousand acres of wheat devoid of anything else are disturbing. Vermont has a scale of farms, forests and villages that balance each other in a way that has been lost elsewhere. In 2009, the National Geographic Society ranked Vermont fifth among the unspoiled great destinations on the planet, and first in the U.S. Not a negligible endorsement.

Not surprisingly, it's a haven for creative types. They come for its beauty and quiet and relative affordability. We were not at that time aware of its problems and downsides. That its admired working landscape is endangered. That it is one of the whitest state in the Union with an aging population. That some of its cities and towns are economically depressed, and that the lack of opportunities drives its young people away.

We were taken with the picture postcard villages. Each with a town green flanked by a general store, a convenience used by residents not just a draw to tourists who want to think they are in a small village; town offices, tiny post office and library, and the requisite spired white church. Each a cliché, and each irresistible. Biking on backcountry roads, we discovered swimming holes and small wilderness lakes, and since I love swimming in lakes and rivers beyond any outdoor activity, these became a powerful draw. Finally, the miraculous fact (at least as it was relayed to us by a less-than-reliable source) that despite all the forests and ferns and damp hidden places, poison ivy does not grow in Vermont. What a wondrous, magical place! All this and no poison ivy! (Which turned out to be untrue.)

Ted, one of the lucky humans not allergic to poison ivy, was not swayed by the lack of it. But listening to me build the case for Vermont, he suspected that my mind was made up.

"Are you trying to convince me or yourself?" he asked after a particularly rhapsodic monologue. "Because your mind is all made up, isn't it?"

Was it? Had I talked myself into it in the effort to convince Ted? Was Vermont really what I wanted?

For the entire winter, we talked and talked about Vermont. Everything we knew we learned from our drives through the dark to and from skiing. Not at all the same as living there, but there was not the luxury of time to spend months trying it out. We determined that we would spend some weekends there in spring, summer and fall.

Spring was late that year, and Vermont's fifth season – mud -- persisted when Central Park was already an island of green. The snow had retreated, leaving the land in crusty layers. The trees still bare, their trunks dark with rivulets. Each footprint left a wound in the saturated earth.

I was certain I had made a terrible mistake coming so early. Why hadn't I waited? Who could find beauty in this gray, sodden landscape? I could see the beauty of rebirth and renewal in every damp branch and stiff white blade of grass. Ted was looking at the here and now, not at a future burst of green life.

And then, he surprised me. We had been married thirty-five years. We could have arguments without either of us saying a word, because I knew what he was thinking and he was wrong, and he knew what I was thinking about what he was thinking, and of course, I was wrong. And still, he surprised me.

"I'm pretty sure we could be happy here," he said. After all, Vermont was relatively familiar. It would be "a change, but not too much of a change." We would be close enough to our son David and our friends to see them regularly. Manhattan would be a manageable drive or train ride. We could add the new to some of the old, gaining much and losing nothing. Simple minded but logical reasoning at the time.

Then, "Let's just do it," he said. "If we make a mistake, we'll make another change. But let's do it soon."

If wishes were horses, fools would ride.

Lake

Each late fall, after the garden is put to bed and before the snow arrives, when it's too cold to bike and the hiking trails are slippery with soaked leaves, Ted offers a solution: "Stop complaining and come with me." The pool is down the hill at the college, convenient, inexpensive, serviceable.

"I can't," I say and he doesn't ask again. It's a decision made months before, a week or two after Labor Day, when I am like that mouse poet in *Frederick*, Leo Lionni's beloved children's book. Instead of hoarding food for winter with the other mice, Frederick sits on the stone wall, thinking. When called to task, he answers that he too is working. He is gathering sunshine, and warmth, and blue skies that he will share with the others in winter's gloom.

Today, the week after Labor Day, is likely the last swim of the season in Glen Lake. And like Frederick, I am gathering colors and sensations for the swimless days ahead.

The sun, unimpeded in a cerulean sky, is caressing in a pleasant but no longer hot glow. The water is also warm, but an exploratory leg into the depths comes up chilled. By next week, or the week after, the surface too will chill and drop, and the water from below, cool throughout the summer, will rise.

The water lies flat and glittering. I ease myself off the rocks. Moving only inches at a time, I am aware of the water line rising along my torso, the chill drowning out the warmth above. When the rocks give out and the mud and plants begin, I dive in, leaving a V-shaped track. The water washes over my face. I am immersed, tasting and smelling water rich in life.

Swimming in a wilderness lake is primal. Often I'm the only one in the water, but even with Ted nearby, swimming is by nature solitary. My head partially submerged, I am deaf to all sounds. The solitude and rhythm encase me in a fluid cocoon. Everything ordinary recedes out of reach. I am weightless. The water drains all worries, annihilates ordinary thought.

Holding my nose (I didn't learn to swim until I was a teenager, and never properly), I force my way under the surface, into a dream world of bluegreen. The daggering light makes the waters translucent. Serpentine plants undulate below me. Corkscrew stems, Medusa curls, giant flat leaves dancing toward the light. I too am dancing in the refracted glow. I too am suffused with the colors and the light. My limbs, stripped of bone, undulate freely. My skin has flaked off and settled in the soft mud. I am almost all water myself.

Coming up, I float serenely, limbs spread, unmoving, the water lapping at the entrance to my ears, its weight pulling on my hair. A band of thin cloud stretches across the deep blue. From the middle of the lake, the western shore appears shadowed, the conifer forest thick and dark. I swim toward the eastern shore where the roots of the cedars and pines curve across the boulders and into the water. There is no wind. The trees are chiseled darkly in the water. I swim into them, rippling their branches and needles. As I reach again into the sky, they settle back into a silent watching.

Much later, I lie on the flat boulder that I have claimed as mine. The water drains out of my hair and skin, taking the wild smell of the lake with it. The sun filters through my eyelids, warms my reconstituting skin.

The images are strung together, a series of moments I can call up in the dentist's chair or crawling through traffic. They will remain pure, undiluted by swimming in a pool. I will be patient through fall and winter, but by late spring I will go to the lake regularly to check on its readiness to receive my body. In early June, there will be a string of unseasonably warm days. Then, when I'm swimming again, my body will remember all that my mind had stored away.

Way Out Where

The realtors had given up on us, and even Ted was wavering, but I remained optimistic. Back in the '80s I had spent a year writing ads and generating media coverage for a large real estate company. The Internet had since changed the industry remarkably, but the euphemisms had remained constant. Brushing up on country properties, I learned to read the listings critically, instantly translating the industry lingo. A "pond" minus any adjectives meant, at best, a vernal pool, at worst, a mosquito infested wetland. Views, also as a stand alone, meant that after cutting a thousand trees there might be a narrow perspective of distant views. Secluded meant impossibly remote and requiring a very long driveway. On the other hand, close to town meant that the property was bisected by a road that carried real traffic by Vermont standards. Easy-on-easy-off a major road… well, that was obvious to anyone.

Armed with this new sophistication and detailed maps, we ventured out on our own. It was quick and efficient. We could look at half a dozen places in a day because the drive told us everything. By the time we reached the "For Sale" sign, we knew that the land was too steep or too narrow, too claustrophobic or too close to the road, too wet or too thickly forested. No more wasted drives to spaghetti lots. No more trudging in mud that would "of course dry up." No more patient walking around pretending that the land had possibilities if only…

The truth, which we ignored as long as possible, was that it wasn't the realtors' fault. Simply, there remain very few large buildable parcels in the southern part of the state. In 2004, when we were searching, the median size of woodland parcels sold fell 45 percent to 17.1 acres, while the median size of open land parcels dropped 29 percent to 5.1 acres. Meanwhile, prices rose 74 percent and 30 percent respectively, partially because the smaller the lot, the higher the per acre price.

While the shortage of land is a problem for those of us looking for it, it's excellent news to those concerned with preserving the state's rural character. A good portion of the land is held in land trusts, preventing development and therefore sales to people like us. Another factor is that state regulations make subdivision a lengthy and expensive process that owners of old family homesteads often can't afford to undertake. And stiff septic regulations can render even very large parcels undevelopable.

Our dream was rapidly eroding. We had searched through mud season and an exceptionally rainy spring. We had watched trees flower and leaf out, and fields turn green then tan with seedheads. Summer had peaked, the days were shrinking, and our drives home in the gathering dark were passed raising questions for which we had no answers.

Ted, having bought into the adventure late, was losing momentum rapidly. It was simply not important enough, he maintained, to "drive ourselves crazy" over it. "Let's regroup and think of something else. I know you will think of many, endless something elses," he finally suggested.

I didn't want to think of anything else. I couldn't think of anything else. I was driven, stubborn, and fortified with irrational hope.

The landscape conspired to sustain my defiance and feed Ted's flagging enthusiasm. It cancelled out the bone-rattling roads with the saturated colors of fall. It overwhelmed the frustration with indigo skies emptied of humid afternoon deluges. The prospect of having to wait out a full winter and another mud season before continuing the search drove me on. The search hardened into an obsession.

I believed. I believed that despite almost three seasons' worth of clear and incontrovertible evidence, the place that existed in our minds also existed just beyond the Internet listings and real estate offices. And there was proof! As we wore out the white sedan on rutted roads, we saw it pulsating in the dulling colors of the canopy, in the airy portals of broad valleys, in the silence that filled the twilight. Our place was waiting in one of the valleys embraced by mountains or on a commanding hilltop.

Ted drove on, waiting for me to come to my senses. He didn't set a time limit, but I knew it would come. We expanded the radius, moving a few miles north, then west, then north again. We spoke about other things now, and took time out for short hikes. Sometimes we biked, thinking it might be easier to meet locals on a bike, who might, in response to our friendly greetings, direct us to the unlisted and perfect land.

It wasn't the actual chats but the preparations for the chats that took time, as the chats turned out to be the shorter part. A well-known Vermont exchange goes like this: "Good morning," the visitor says cheerfully. The response is a sedate nod. "Do you know how to get to Point A?" This time the response is verbal. "Yup," followed by silence.

By our experience, this is a gross exaggeration with a kernel of truth. Once we were living in Vermont, people turned out to be surprisingly open to conversation and slow-growing friendships. But during those months when we were strangers, our attempts at engaging the locals met with little success. I have spent more than two decades in public relations and journalism, and Ted has been in sales and marketing most of his career. This vast combined experience in human relations should have made us competent at ordinary conversation. But our most charming overtures were met with polite silence, with sedate head nodding, and with one-word answers. Rarely with a question, which is what drives ordinary conversation.

We would walk into the general store or a small diner. We'd haul ourselves up to the few seats at the counter, and offer a bright smile and a cheery greeting. These would elicit silent nods. Undeterred, we'd latch onto the weather, a legitimate topic of conversation anywhere and especially so in Vermont, where it's spectacularly unpredictable.

"Is this cold/wind/rain/heat normal for this time of year?" we'd ask, since this would immediately establish us as not from these parts. Now, in other parts of the country, there might be a detailed answer, followed by a question such as "Where you folks from?"

Not in Vermont. The common response would take a minute or more to arrive, and it would be something like "Well… you never know. It is some years."

This would effectively end the weather portion of the exchange. We'd have to quickly find a new topic with more promise, one that would circuitously lead to the information we were seeking. A compliment on the coffee or the 27 flavors of ice cream, designed to create a new opening onto what might lead to a conversation about the town and ultimately to real estate, would flounder.

We took care to brush up on local news. Once, we learned about a murder of passion that took place the night before in the very next town. Here was our chance to show – through knowledge of the details and understanding of the social forces operating locally – what we thought was self-evident: that we were already nearly part of the woof and fabric of the place.

"Do *we* know what will happen to the children?" I asked a woman whom I had engaged in what I loosely interpreted as a friendly exchange, meaning that she had responded to my mention of the flowering crabapples in seductive bloom that lined the street.

"No."

"I hope they have family who will take them in," I said, adding that these poor children needed a familiar place during this trauma.

She nodded, in agreement I thought, but then maybe it was a dismissive nod saying that what I said was self-evident and stating the obvious required no response.

After living in Vermont for some years, we began to understand that Vermonters come in two categories: the natives and the transplants or flatlanders. With the transplants, we could forge quick social ties. The natives, we learned, respond differently. They are generally talkative and outgoing, knowledgeable and helpful in the extreme, tolerant and fair. But they are used to a different approach, especially from strangers like us. It was up to us to learn their ways. Saying nothing and waiting for them to speak first is often the best approach.

During the search, however, we remained mystified. Despite the sunny opening moves and clever verbal maneuverings, the most we ever learned was that there was a real estate office in town, which we already knew, or in the next town, ditto, and they may know something there. They didn't.

The search lengthened into fall. We watched in dismay as in the general stores the flip-flops were replaced by snow boots. Frantic, we made offers on two parcels that represented serious compromises. To our astonishment, we lost both to others who bid above the asking price. This cost nights of lost sleep and days of frustrated wonderment. We couldn't even get what we didn't really want! Should we just give up? Or give up for this year and wait for next? Would it be more likely that we'd be priced out by then? Would we lose the money set aside for the land to some emergency? Would all the land be bought and sold, closed and gone? Should we look in New Hampshire or Maine, or even in upstate New York? Should we just stay put?

By late October, I too was readying myself to accept defeat. In a last-ditch effort, moving beyond the latest circle we'd drawn on the map, I studied the fuzzy photos of a forty-acre property. The price was beyond our reach, but it had been listed for many months. At any rate, it looked as if it might have some views and it wasn't near any road that looked major.

It was, in fact, more than three miles from the nearest town, starting out on a respectable paved road with sidewalks that bisected a college campus. But where the pavement ended, the road was obliterated by a dust storm that blew up with every passing car. (We were assured that rain settles the dust, which turned out to be true. When it rains.) The town recycling center and a slate operation, neither a desirable neighbor, followed the college. A small, unkempt but powerfully odorous dairy farm straddled both sides as the road wound up the hill. After that, widely spaced houses and woods alternated. At the top of the hill, a tall wire fence, mostly hidden by maples, enclosed a dying orchard. This was the property we had come to see.

A bent cattle gate and a large sign announced that "Trespassers Will Be Shot!" The gate was tied with heavy ropes that were meant to stay tied, so we hauled ourselves up and jumped down the other side, landing hard on aging knees. On the right sat an ancient, listing barn with a deep mud floor and missing doors. A mountain of deteriorating wooden crates rose by it. Ted walked over, looked back at me, and shook his head. "Not worth the time," he was saying. I looked at him and shook my shoulders. "You just never know," I was signaling. We walked up a rutted path, most of which consisted of a rock face. It was there to climb and the morning sun was warm. We expected nothing.

Some five hundred feet to the top, with grieved looking apple trees stretching away on both sides. The path was no longer visible. Instead, a steep mountain's undulating profile was sketched against the eastern sky, the last of the fall colors blazing on its upper flanks. To the south, a pasture rose slightly before the land fell away in a series of low hills. A narrow band of Lake Champlain and another, closer lake glittered in the west, with a series of lavender Adirondack peaks rising beyond. A small forest and more mountains hovered in the north. Above it all, the entire blue heavens rose in a sheltering bowl.

I sat down, overcome by the drama. The barren hilltop underneath me was covered with jumbled piles of dead apple trees. Some had been herded into mounds, but most just lay around like the bleached bones of prehistoric creatures.

Before we had time to consider what all the destruction meant, we heard what were, unmistakable even to our city ears, pounding hooves.

”What’s that?” I screamed, looking at Ted in terror and continuing to sit inanely.

“Get up!” he yelled, pulling my arm nearly out of its socket.

From between the rows of apple trees, a couple dozen cows and a few bulls were rushing at us. Ted picked up a small trunk and waved it about shouting, a Neanderthal defending his woman, who was pounding down the hill and scrambling up the gate, followed by the animals, which were followed by Ted, who was screaming at me to climb faster, as if I needed a cheerleader in my escape from certain death.

For a dizzy moment I hung on top of the gate, one leg on each side as the gate lazily swung open, releasing its twin from the ropes that held them together. I watched, horrified, as the cows and bulls calmly walked through the gate while I hung on it screaming, certain they would pursue me up the gate as I’ve read bears pursue their prey up trees.

Instead, the cattle dispersed up and down the road and into neighbors’ yards. We dispersed to the car, locking the doors. My head was in my lap, my breath ragged. Ted was watching the cattle discovering their new world.

“We should go to the real estate office,” he finally announced.

Heading down the road toward civilization, Ted became philosophical, insisting he had not actually been afraid.

“They were not out to attack us, they just thought we meant that food was coming,“ he explained, as if he had been handling cattle since the day he was weaned.

“Food is in the eye of the beholder,” I answered, “and I wasn’t about to stand around and see which kind they meant.”

“It was shocking,” I said, finally catching my breath, “the speed at which cows can run.”

I’d never seen them do anything but chew, moving ponderously if at all. I was developing a healthy respect for cows, even more so for bulls.

Bursting breathlessly into the real estate office, we spilled the details of the dramatic escape to a baffled woman, who was joined by two others as our tale progressed. One of them left to find the animals' owner.

"So. Are you interested in the property?" the first woman asked.

We looked at each other stupidly and answered in unison.

"Yes, yes, and oh, yes," I think we said.

We were assured that the animals would be contained and we could safely return to the property. With the realtor.

"It's too good to be true," Ted said on the drive back.

"You're probably right," I agreed. "It's been for sale for months."

"So what's the catch?" he asked, a purely rhetorical question.

By the time we walked through the now open gate, the sun was right above us, turning the Taconics a pale blue and bleaching the colors out of the face to the east, which we learned was named Birdseye Mountain. After the first hour, realizing this was to be an extended visit, the realtor left. Walking the perimeter of forty acres can be long, given that it adds up to about fifteen city blocks or three quarters of a mile. Especially long when trudging over undulating earth and through nose-high, rough grass, and higher goldenrod. Much like walking through a shallow sea with a strong undertow.

Except for a steep area of young woods of mostly birches and maples, the acreage consisted of old semi-dwarf Red Delicious and Macintosh apple trees. Alas, most were dead or dying, and of those still standing, many could be knocked down with a healthy kick. In the bottom third of the land, where the winds were of the valley instead of mountains, the trees were larger, alive with many fruits, imperfect but intensely flavored. Here the world was close and protective, the sky glimpsed between the trees in familiar shreds. A large secret garden offering a wealth of fruit that continued to grow without human intervention.

It wasn't until after we'd bought the land that we learned about the sad history of apple orchards in Vermont. How all but a handful had been abandoned when China became the prime apple supplier. How the climate was unsuited to organic apple farming, the humidity a haven to mildew and a host of diseases. And, too late, how orchards were a liability, reducing the value of land.

But none of this would have made a difference. Here, finally, was real land. Large enough. Wild enough. Peaceful. Private. And with the best views this side of the Rockies. We were rapidly falling under the spell of the place.

We made an offer that very weekend, above what we'd planned to spend but well below the asking price. I was troubled. It was two-and-half times more than our current house had cost us, and there was no house on it! I was worried about whether we were overpaying, setting ourselves up to be land poor, whether we'd ever be able to sell it if we needed the money, whether we were missing some tragic fault that was obvious to anyone who knew anything about land. We hadn't discovered any downside that would explain why it hadn't sold, except that it had been poorly marketed and overpriced. Still, there was plenty of fodder for night terrors.

Our offer was accepted, which turned the nagging anxieties into full-blown panic. But we couldn't find any reason not to forge ahead. In any case, we were already madly, deeply, hopelessly in love, blind to faults.

Then, weeks of delay while the seller tried to locate missing documents and fight off creditors. He had half a dozen liens against the property, the major one from an ex-wife who wasn't kindly disposed and threatened to stop the sale.

I remained convinced that despite the setbacks we were destined to have this land. I'd walked nearly every square foot of it, climbed its trees and eaten its apples. I'd taken a tally of its grasses and wildflowers. I'd watched the sun rise one morning in Birdeye's cleft and set that evening over the Adirondacks. We had located the perfect house site, had already designed the low-slung log house, and worked out the landscaping with high-bush blueberries and wildflower meadows.

The feud with the lien-holders dragged on. It was time to light a fire. Ten days, we said, before the deal is off. For good. We were so firm I started to believe we meant it, and began to distance myself from the dream. Maybe gale force winds pound regularly and no house could be built to withstand them. Perhaps the sun, so benign in October, is a withering presence in June. Despite the negative laboratory results, the water and earth could be toxic for generations from the chemicals sprayed on the trees. Somebody told us the area is prone to hail storms. And as always, as with every property we'd considered, there were the unknowns: what if the adjoining fifty acres are subdivided into ten-acre lots? Or an industrial wind farm rises overnight on that scalloped mountain face?

Arriving at the lawyer's office for the closing on time, we were apparently much too early. The real estate agent arrived soon after, but the three lawyers and the seller came in one by one over the next hour. Annoyed, squeezed into a tiny office with people who took no note of the momentousness of the occasion, waiting for the waivers on the liens to arrive one by one, the process took nearly four hours. It was long past lunch when we walked out with the deed, which clearly stated that the property as delineated on the town map was ours.

Rather than the planned celebratory meal, we picked up pizza and rushed to our hill. Why waste time in a restaurant when we could be in our own Eden? By the time we were done with setting up camp, the sun had set and blasts of wind whipped at the tent flaps.

The wind died down when the moon reached a point directly above us. We left the tent and went back out to sit on beach chairs on the smooth granite of our hilltop, the remains of a bottle of champagne between us.

"When we have the house built, we'll observe a daily cocktail hour at sunset," I suggested.

"Sure," Ted agreed readily.

Then we laid out the rest of our lives in our new domain. Our days would be full and productive and exhausting. Half the day we'd toil on the apple trees, the vegetable garden, the cutting garden, the woodpile, the mowing and general maintenance. The other half would be devoted to paid work. A satisfying combination of physical labor and intellectual pursuits. Winter, of course, would demand a new schedule. And when we'd be too old to do much else, we'd still have plenty to watch: the movements of the sun and moon, the ever-changing sky, the unfolding weather that could be seen moving toward us from a hundred miles away.

"Not bad for a couple of greenhorns," mused Ted, waving his arms to encompass the whole of creation, which we felt was ours by virtue of its all being visible from our hill.

The moon passed over us and began its slow descent. Heads thrown back to the sky, we sat long enough for ghosts to creep out. They came, my ancestors, rudely wedging themselves into my plans for a perfect life. They had lived for a thousand years in villages or small towns, hating the mud they had to trudge through to bargain over rags or potatoes, wrapping themselves against the damp, the poverty, the centuries of persecution.

"Eh, toiling on apple trees? You *meshuga*? What you know from apple trees?"

"You will grow flowers? Sell flowers? Huh," another croaked derisively. "Since when we make a living with flowers? Why not with reciting poetry, maybe?"

"And what will you write from hereeee?" a shaky voice rasped. "From heeere you can't write notin because you don't know notin so far from civilization. On a mountain!"

The city was their refuge, where they could work and worship, where they felt a small measure of safety among their own people. What was I doing here, a nomad traveling to this wild, open, unprotected place, sleeping in a tent on the ground, sitting outside in the damp night air?

Even my mother, who loved nature and words, who in Auschwitz fed herself with rhyming stanzas about remembered springs and my grandmother's fluffy golden chala, joined the chorus of dissent. She didn't speak, but her gaze was baffled, sad for me.

They all crowded behind me, their breath reeking of herring and onions, their beards and long coats stale with indoor air. Their thin voices wrapped themselves around me, joining the wisps of smoke from the fire, insinuating themselves into my throat, choking off my future. "No!" I shouted silently. "I will do this because I can! Because I can finally, finally put down roots. Because I feel safe. I will not be herded away with a single suitcase. I can surround myself with what I love and it won't be torn from me."

"Go away!" I thought, half awake now. "You all have paid dearly. For twenty centuries you have endured so I can live free from terror."

Staring into the moon, I shut them out. The moon was bright enough to blind, so it was some time before I noticed that the very air in front of me was pricked with brilliant stars, huge stars, magnificent and rising from the earth on huge dark limbs. The real eyes of the very real cows and bulls, coming closer as the fire retreated to smoldering coals, quickly displaced my ancestors.

I made a swift strategic escape to the tent, furious at Farmer Bob who had been so gracious when we asked that he remove his animals for the weekend, send them away on some new Fresh Air experience. And here they were again, not openly menacing this time, but not peaceful, distant companions like the deer either. They meandered off after a time, but the bulls were staying put. Leaving Ted outside to build up the fire and keep watch, I was grateful to retreat into the defenseless female role. I am not generally fearful but have an irrational fear of animals, even dogs. The cows were bigger than dogs, and the bulls presented an altogether different plane of fear.

Ted reported next day that he had not been afraid. And despite his protestations to the contrary, he seemed to have enjoyed his vigil. No man is so removed from our human origins that he would find keeping a fire going and brandishing tree limbs in the night less than thrilling.

One more glorious weekend before fall wound down into a gray chill. We spent it showing the land to our children, who flew and drove from distant cities. I forbade them to turn around until after we had reached the summit so they too could be stunned as we had been. I wanted them to love it at first sight, to have it become a fulfillment of their own still unformed needs.

We relived that first sight through their eyes, as we would in coming years through a sometimes overwhelming stream of family and friends, most of whom wouldn't come until assured that indoor plumbing was in place.

Having spent the previous years at college in Colorado, Gabriel was shocked by how Western the landscape was.

"It's that mountain," he proclaimed, pointing to Birdseye, rising perpendicular against the blue. "And this big sky."

"It's, it's ... unbelievable," Daniela, the family poet, lost for words, summed up, turning slowly. Within minutes, she found her voice, and proceeded to list every attribute while the others nodded in silent agreement.

Then, without a word, she disappeared. Like me, she sought solitude. After a long time, we heard cows lowing and convinced they were attacking her, I rushed away in mad pursuit. I found her curled into the long grass in the deepest part of the orchard, asleep, the cows safely tucked into a distant corner.

David trotted alongside in his quiet manner. He was full of rare smiles, planning mountain bike routes, happy at being part of this family adventure.

Gabriel worried about how we'd handle the thousands of trees. A born leader, he began organizing the labor into manageable projects and making lists of machinery we'd have to buy. Having finished the planning, he looked wistfully out over the land, remarking that this would be "the most incredible playground for little kids. You could let them out in the morning and they could return whenever they wanted, and with the fence all around, you'd never need to worry." I responded that it would be up to the three of them to populate this land with children. It was not an opportunity a Jewish mother of three adults, even young ones, could pass up.

November

Mid November, 2009.

The sun shows itself for the first time in six days.

I'd spent the best part of the day holed up with laptop and books, sipping tea, thinking black thoughts. About how I've watched the bobolinks leave, the monarchs drift away, then the geese and, finally, even the nondescript little brown birds are suddenly missed. Only the crows streak across the leaden sky, and an occasional red-tailed hawk to vary their solid blackness.

Just the previous week, the trees had held enough color to give the lie to November. A weekend of wind and rain had stripped them clean. The multi-colored curtain was shredded. Now horses in the neighboring field stand clear against the skeletal hedgerow.

Trying to cheer up, I remember that we'll soon gain an hour. But what does it mean? Longer night or day? Time is a trick to divide the seamless day, as artificial as those straight lines drawn on maps by cartographers, following the exigencies of politics, ignoring the demands of landscapes and cultures.

I live by the sun. I'm at my post in the lounge chair in the living room every morning, waiting for it to emerge from behind Birdseye.

Instead, the dark turns into a murky light. Often, we are an island in an ocean of clouds that reach to the hem of the lawn.

November in Vermont has the fewest sunny days in the year, about one in three. Which means that more than twenty November days are sunless.

When the sun shines, the flies revive. Infuriating, crawling up every surface, droning with dull and horrible persistence, dying outside every glass surface. The flies lie in spread-out torpor on the floors, waiting for their demise. They stay put as I sweep them out. Large black spiders wander in blatantly whenever a door is opened. They spin no webs. Utterly useless in catching the flies. Fat woolybears crowd the porches. Thin brown worms plaster themselves on the stones where they dry out, an ineffective stab at survival.

I'm reading about redwoods, against whose time a human lifetime shrinks to a flicker. Even against the maples in the hedgerow. The conifers we planted for a windbreak will still be in their early teens when we're gone.

With that thought, I force myself out of the chair.

I walk the fields, searching for water. We have two wells rich in hard, icy water, pumped up from the bedrock hundreds of feet below. Just one supplies more than we need. But the water I want has nothing to do with need. I want water I can look at, sit by unmoving, becoming part of the landscape, observing the animals that come to drink. Surface water of any size, a small pond, a slow stream with a tiny waterfall that would bubble up in the spring, a miniature fountain. Even a vernal pool would complete this Eden.

In truth, I can observe animals from anywhere. Birds fly up in chittering clouds as I walk in spring and early summer. Frogs regularly end up indoors, where, thinking they're lizards, they try to climb the walls. Mice and an occasional hedgehog hide in the porch corners. Deer saunter up and down the hills, willfully ignoring our waving arms.

But something there is in humans that craves a body of water. We are, after all, two-thirds water, like the earth. Studies have shown that people's ideal landscape for habitation is on a hill, with forest behind, an open savannah-like view to the front, and a lake or river in the foreground. This preference goes beyond aesthetics. A forest provides protection, an open view makes intruders visible, and the water, like medieval moats around castles, creates a barrier. This kind of landscape is also typical of Africa, where humans first evolved.

We have woods and fields and long views, but no visible water. Even Vermont's infamous fifth season -- mud -- hardly exists on our hill. The melting snow and spring rains drain quickly down the hill. But our elderly neighbor mentioned a marshy area to the west and he should know since his family had once owned this land.

So I walk the land this late fall afternoon looking for water.

The silence that emanates from the earth and the leafless trees and shrunken flowers speaks of a complex chemistry, an intricate, secret readying for a new season.

The shorter days of fall signal a breakdown of the chlorophyll that gives plants their green color, masking the other colors always present in leaves. As the chlorophyll leaches out, the yellows, oranges and reds of the carotenoids are exposed, giving us the spectacle of fall.

At the same time, a barrier of cells forms at the base of each leaf stalk. In response to lowering temperatures, decreasing day lengths or light intensity, the cells near the barrier are broken down by enzymes. Wind and rain then easily break the remaining connecting strands and the leaf falls.

With the leaves gone, next spring's leaf and flower buds are revealed, packed into a protective sheath of bud scales. A hormone switches off all activity in the bud until spring, when the hormone becomes increasingly dilute and the buds burst open. With our short growing season, this "head start" system enables woody plants to grow rapidly in the spring and to complete their annual growth cycle before winter descends again.

A clever adaptation and a subtle miracle.

Now though, death stalks the land. The night's frost killed millions.

It wilted the leaves of the wildflowers and turned their stems into jellied messes. The grasses rise stiffly yellow out of the debris of summer. Even the proud chard in the vegetable bed lies prone on the hardened earth.

It's the animals whose absence is most obvious. The travelers had left, flying or crawling away. The year-round residents had retreated. The ants, bees and wasps, which have become steadily more sluggish as the temperature dropped, have disappeared from sight. All are in hiding, their life force on hold. Unless they're all in the house, in which case their life force becomes my preoccupation.

Still, some life, denying the change, continues. Frosted raspberries hang on, their juice the essence of sweetness in the dying season. Shiny black buckthorn berries, the clubs of sumac, and the bright red winterberries are holding out the promise of food for the remaining birds.

After an hour of rambling, I give up on seeing water. I am ready to accept water-loving plants. Cattails, if only I could find them, would be an unmistakable sign. So would the invasive phragmites, a reed that of course I don't want on my land, but at least I'd know. Even purple loosestrife would be an acceptable clue.

Soon I forget what I'm looking for. I'm walking now for the pleasure of walking, of moving slowly over the land, alert to whatever lies in it, hidden until I open my eyes properly.

There is more living matter beneath the surface than upon it. Several million bacteria in an average square yard of soil. If you add up the microbial, invertebrate, and vertebrate life underground, under each acre is a biomass equivalent to ten draft horses.

But I only see the large things. There is the desolation of lush growth, dried and frozen. The chattering goldenrod stalks form a forest. Queens Anne's lace retains its graceful shape and easy nature, letting me travel through it without it putting out thorns or leaving sticky seeds. I spot a large fallen poplar, its branches still retaining leaves that have died without turning and have forgotten to fall off. Already, dozens of new poplars, thin and wiry, some with multiple trunks and towering above their cousins, crowd on either side of the fallen trunk. Rank opportunists.

I sit to rest on the smooth trunk and pick up a milkweed pod. For a plant, milkweed has been controversial, sparking debate over whether it's a weed or a desirable plant. But one thing is certain: milkweed has a heroic place in American history.

It was used as a kapok substitute during World War II. Kapok – a soft, cottony material from the kapok tree – was used to fill "Mae West" life jackets, but the supply was cut off by Japan's control of Java, one of the main sources. Milkweed floss – waterproof and buoyant – was substituted. Wartime pamphlets encouraged "School children of America! Help save your father's, brothers', and neighbors' lives by collecting milkweed pods." The campaign furnished some two million pounds of milkweed floss to the armed services in one year. An estimated eleven million pounds of milkweed were collected by the end of World War II.

Another certain thing: milkweed, being the sole food of the monarch butterfly caterpillar, is no weed. Even if it were ugly and selfish, which it isn't, it would hold an honored place on our hill.

The pod in my hand is closed tight. I pry open its dry husk and am lost in admiration. Here, in this pod, are maybe a hundred seeds, each a tiny parachute, each securely wrapped in a coat of tissue, topped with iridescent white streamers, designed to fly great distances on the slightest breeze. But what really matters are the seeds in the pod before they are scattered. Because a milkweed pod full of seeds is the most strikingly beautiful piece of work, each half a perfect mirror image of the other, each brown seed and its glossy tail perfectly lined up, layer upon layer of high design and superb engineering, the magic of procreation revealed.

It really doesn't need to be so beautiful, does it? But it is. And it suffices.

Forty Acres and a Cabin

We needed something to live in until the house was built. Something small and simple, primitive even, for weekends and vacations. That first winter was spent investigating the building of a log cabin, called a "camp" in Vermont and commonly used for hunting.

I perused huge, gorgeous books with photo spreads of unique, custom-built log cabins, some larger than the house in which we raised our three children. I salivated over every photo, each unabashed eye candy, each a dream of unattainable craftsmanship and design. Ted did his homework on the Internet, which was less fun but more pragmatic since maybe we could actually afford one of the cabins sold there.

Maybe not, we thought, after looking at the costs involved. Worse, none looked like the photos. They weren't even cabins, just huge piles of precut lumber with detailed plans that were so simple and clear that "anyone who can use a hammer and screwdriver can assemble the cabin in a weekend."

"Count me out," I stated unequivocally. "I can't ever get a nail into anything without bending it in several directions first."

Ted, who is generally the half empty-glass type, had vague ideas about how he could do it himself, maybe, if, assuming, in case, if only… Then, into the mix of uncertainties, he added some friends who might help, friends who we both knew would never drive to Vermont to spend a weekend struggling with such an overwhelming project.

I'm a hopeless romantic in certain areas. I love the concept of rugged self-sufficiency and admire competence in any craft, from fixing a dripping faucet to knitting mittens that fit. (Any pair I knit mysteriously turns out not only differently sized but also wildly divergent in shape.) Certainly, building a house or even turning a pile of precut, numbered lumber into a cabin is admirable. I've always desperately wanted to be among those capable beings who can do things for themselves. In fact, I can easily understand how intelligent women regularly run off with their contractors and carpenters. But I was not going to participate in anything as irrational as Ted building a cabin.

It took less than a week to convince him that it might be best to let a professional tackle the building. Clear evidence that I was right.

We contacted cabin companies, which referred us to people who could also assemble them. But as the numbers came in, it became clear that these guys weren't looking for a weekend or two of work to complement their income. They saw this job as the very income they had been wanting, just what would make it possible for them to enjoy an extra long hunting season. We presented a terrific opportunity to make a lot of money in a short time off naïve city folk with greenbacks to burn. Why else would people hire someone to build a camp? By definition, a camp is a roughhewn place that you build yourself, maybe with your brother or your hunting buddies. You hire builders to build a house. Therefore, it made sense to charge for building a house.

"That big tent we borrowed from your sister wasn't so bad," I ventured after the third estimate arrived.

"We could build a platform for it, like they do in the national parks," I continued as Ted glared.

"Well then, you come up with a better solution," I snapped.

"You know what would be logical?" he responded, without missing a beat. Apparently he had been waiting for just such an opportunity to share his brainstorm.

"No. What?"

"A trailer."

"You mean like that cute one at the bottom of the road? With the wraparound porch?"

This was a yes-no question, but he took a long while to reply.

"Not exactly. No. I meant an old trailer, one with a dying or dead engine, would be perfect."

And he continued elaborating, ignoring my stricken face.

"A rusty, corroded, moldy trailer. Perfect, and we could add a port-a-potty," I said. "The two together would be so romantic."

"Well, not romantic, but you know it would be sensible. We could get rid of it after the house is built."

It was, undeniably, sensible. And a desecration. A dilapidated metal structure, here on our verdant Vermont hill! Horrible! Unthinkable!

At least it was so at the time. After several years of living here, I've learned to appreciate the practicality Ted alluded to. Many hardworking, resourceful Vermonters live in trailers, and while not rusty hulks, most don't have wraparound porches either. Working a job or even two at minimum wage and raising a family doesn't allow many housing options. Trailers are private, warm, clever, affordable. I fully understand their value. If I had to choose between a cramped apartment or a trailer surrounded by grass, I'd surely choose the latter.

And still, I must admit, I do not like them.

As the trailer discussion deteriorated into a series of accusations of sheer heartlessness and worse, total lack of aesthetic principles, countered by defensiveness, and finally into the "'alwayses" and the "nevers" that signal dead ends in marital arguments, we came to a dead end. Fortunately, in the interim, cabin companies had found us. One was a small factory in southeastern Vermont that specialized in outbuildings, including three fully built cabins of various sizes. We spent a sunny late winter day, brilliant ski slopes mocking from every direction, trudging through the frozen mud between the cabins.

The cabin we chose was their largest at 12 by 36 feet, including a tiny porch.. It wasn't custom built, and since it was sided with pine board, not really a log cabin. We upgraded to extra windows and an additional glass-paned door. The peeled logs supporting the porch roof had to do for authenticity.

We were ecstatic. A real dwelling with windows that we could open and shut, wide plank floors, and a wooden screen door that banged shut with that sound that is the essence of remembered summers. I imagined ethnic rugs with primary colors and my huge moose mugs hanging from the shelves that comprised the "kitchen."

On the way home, the subject of water, heat and toilet came up. Heat was simple. The smallest wood stove would keep us flushed with warmth in the tiny space. Water presented real challenges. How to get the water up from the existing well without electricity to drive a pump? And where would the water go once up?

Facilities were another puzzle. An outhouse that matched the cabin was part of the purchase. On my insistence, a sickle moon was carved into the door, making it a proper privy. The views to the outside would be spectacular, but what exactly would we put inside?

Whom could we ask? Not anyone we knew nor anyone in Vermont, where the poorest trailers have running water and electricity. The people who sold us the cabin and outhouse had no answers. They confessed that the cabins were normally placed next to existing houses with flush toilets. But they were selling outhouses, right? Not exactly. They were building one for us, but it wasn't one of their hottest selling items.

We divided the task. Since I was "obsessed" about a toilet, finding one became my job. Ted was in charge of securing a stove and getting the water out of the well, I in charge of storing it. Trolling the Internet, I came across survivalist sites, which offered everything we needed for life in the woods, from water barrels and hand pumps to battery-operated lanterns and solar radios.

The toilet remained an intractable issue. We yo-yoed for weeks between a composting toilet or a plain old pit. The first was expensive and was reported to be far from odor free, as claimed. The other was, well, an odorous hole in the ground. Plus I was terrified of the black widow spiders and other dark, unknown creatures that would lurk in such a pit, just waiting for someone like me to innocently settle onto the seat.

One of the cabin books featured a cabinetmaker who had built a beautiful cabin on an island in an Adirondack lake and put in a marine toilet, which he claimed was a masterpiece of clever design.

I called him. The conversation did not start off well.

After brief introductions, I came to the point.

"I wanted to talk with you about your wonderful toilet."

"Really?" he asked, his voice rising dangerously.

"Yes, we're building a cabin, well, having a cabin built." I hated to admit it but didn't want to get into a conversation about construction. "And so, we need a toilet."

That seemed to put him at ease, and he proceeded to elucidate his choice by providing some context, which amounted to a doctoral dissertation on the chemistry of human waste and the physics of its disposal. What I gleaned was that this cunning toilet separated the liquids from the solids, thus eliminating odor entirely. (As we later discovered, since it didn't entirely separate one from the other, neither did it entirely eliminate odors.)

I had had enough. We ordered the marine toilet.

Armed with orange flags, we came to pick out a site for the cabin. We stomped around until we agreed that the top of the rutted road once used for the orchard offered the best views. We paced and measured and placed flags in the corners, which by the third corner were never straight. When we had what seemed close enough to a rectangle, we paced the distance to the outhouse site, figuring out its orientation. You want the door to face you as you reach it, but you don't want people looking into it from inside the cabin. You want it close in winter, but not too close. You want a straight line, so you can memorize it easily for those overcast nights. You want decent soil, so you can plant the traditional hedge of lilacs along the path, a practical and beautiful way to mask odors.

We kept stopping to drink and stare and lie in the spring sun. When we thought we were done, we realized we had forgotten to decide on the cabin's orientation. Where should the porch be? Facing south for warmth? East for the sunrise, or west for the sunset? With too little glass for solar heating, we chose the sunrise. Then I went to the woods to look for pine seedlings to transplant for a wind screen.

When I stepped out of the woods toward the bottom of the hill, I forgot all about the pines. Because below and in front was a vista I'd never seen before, a whole novel aspect of our land. Below a steep drop stretched an undulating valley, the tops of the apple trees arranged in straight rows across it. Beyond this valley of trees, the Adirondack giants rose, still in their snow-covered splendor.

We could put the vegetable garden here, I thought, and create a reason to spend a chunk of each day in that spot. With a swinging bench for admiring the prolific vegetation and a cold glass of wine.

Do such lives exist?

Not for us, we agreed, laughing about our future "retirement."

"Let others relax on Florida beaches or golf in gated communities," I said. "We'll have better things to do, right?"

"Right. Between the daily quota of trees to cut, chop and stack; the snowshoeing up to the house and down to the car, and ..."

"And the large vegetable garden. And maybe we'll grow flowers to sell. You know I love farmers markets."

"Right, that too, and what about all the berry bushes and nut trees?

"Which have to be harvested and preserved."

We'll either live very long and healthy lives or die young from overwork was the consensus.

And then it's May. I walk in the sun-lit gaps on the sidewalks through Manhattan's frenetic crowds. The hill beckons. I know the mud had receded and the apple trees are covered with tight pink buds. I ache to be there when the buds unfurl as much as a mother wishes to witness her child's first steps. We are ready for spring on the hill, in the cabin.

But the cabin isn't ready as promised. The very pleasant girl says it's actually ready, except that.

"The wrong size windows were sent," she explains in a tiny, sing-song voice.

"Some of them are the right size," she corrects herself.

"How many are the wrong size?" I ask.

There is no straightforward answer.

"Well, some are almost the right size, so I think, maybe, they can be fitted ..." she trails off.

"Fitted? How?"

"Can you please hold on? I'll get Peter."

Peter is the owner, a scowling young man, spare in frame and words. When we met him, he had nodded at us and turned the brim of his cap to the side. I took that as a greeting, and smiled. He did not return the smile.

Now on the phone, I can tell he is again not smiling.

"The windows came in wrong," he confirms, and stops. Clearly, it's going to be a Q&A session, and the As will be curt.

"I know that and it's too bad. So when can you get the right ones?"

"In a couple of weeks."

"Does that mean two or many weeks?"

"Probably more than two, but hard to tell."

"Could it be six or eight weeks?"

"It could." And that is that. No apologies.

"That would mean we'd lose out on all of spring, maybe even part of summer," I can't help wailing. "Do you understand what this means to us? We paid you the full amount up front, and you promised ..."

I have to stop. Tears are a real possibility, and weakness would not work on Peter.

Given the stony silence emanating from the other end, I feel it appropriate to revert to my default mode: aggressive Manhattanite. It works. Although no specific promises are made, Peter's austere composure is showing signs of fraying. He mistakenly lets on that getting the right windows quickly would cost him. I take this to mean that the windows came in wrong because they had been ordered wrong.

After a week of email exchanges and phone conversations that alternate between sweet entreaties and firm demands, the cabin is miraculously ready. It was made clear that I was expected to feel guilty for costing the company extra money. I feel nothing but elation. The cabin is due to arrive the following Saturday.

The truck, pulling the cabin on a flatbed, can be heard on the dirt road long before it stops and all four occupants step out to survey the steep and curving drive to the top of the knoll. There is much shaking of heads and mutterings, followed by raised arms and voices. I know my place. Away from these Vermont boys. Let them be the competent men they surely are. I am not wanted, and in fact, have nothing to offer. But there is our cabin, our perfect little home, where we are going to cook and sleep that night. And it's in danger of being whisked away right under my distressed gaze, for who knows how long!

Ted walks down to talk to the guys, legs spread, like a cowboy. I sit on the grass, stiff with tension, wondering at this transformation in my husband.

This division of labor seems effective, because two of the men get back in the truck and it starts moving again while the others hop about, gesticulating wildly in front of the slowly moving truck. I too am up, moving in place.

The truck stops and everyone gets out again. All five walk to the barn and return with the one small chainsaw. I am guessing they need to remove a couple of trees to make room for the truck and cabin. This is acceptable in the scheme of things, and I relax, certain now that the cabin will be brought to its resting place, since the way back down seems as confounding as the way up.

Once on top, the cabin's chassis is removed and before noon it's placed on cement blocks. Soon, as soon as it's level, I will be able to open the door and walk inside.

The outhouse is unloaded, but even lying on its side it looks all wrong. Wrong shape and no moon cutout in the door, which itself seems far too short. Stood up properly, it's clear that we'd have to crawl in.

I point this out to the men, but they regard me silently. Why would anything make sense in this bizarre setup, they surely wonder. But they can't ignore the obvious fact that the outhouse is not meant for even the shortest humans. They call Peter, who after some on-site research confirms that the structure is a rather large chicken coop. The outhouse will be delivered the following week.

This minor catastrophe barely mars our elation. We drag the steps to the front and climb onto the tiny porch. The sun glows through the stained glass inset. Inside, the aroma of virgin pine is intoxicating. The views, framed by the small windows, are each a rich palette of intense green, lavender and blue, weaving a triptych in each wall.

We set up the camp stove and boil water. The reconstituted split pea soup is superb, as is the bread toasted directly on the flame. The sleeping bags are positioned on the floor at the far end of the "open floor plan." We are in them before the light fades.

A year later, a neighbor wanted a cabin like ours for use as a guest house. We happily referred him to Peter. But alas, he had stopped building cabins. When, the neighbor asked. The answer was, pretty much after ours. I chose not to think about that confluence of events.

Sassafras

Since the first walk in these fields and woods, I have tried to know and name what I see. Eight years later, this naming of things, this taxonomic yearning continues to drive me mad.

When I know the name, I can't always retrieve it. Often it pops out of my swampy memory bank days later. When I don't know it, but should, it's defeating. When I can't realistically be expected to know it, there's hope in the guidebooks. But this also often ends in frustration. Because after a protracted search, when I finally zero in on the very plant; the one with the same rosette of leaves and furry stem, the flower with the same number of pale yellow petals blooming in the early spring. When I'm certain I'm finally deciphering the outrageously complex key to these books… what do I find? That the plant grows only on mountain peaks or bogs or is a woodland ephemeral. Without any doubt, it cannot grow in this meadow.

Why this fixation, this mania of putting a name to every tree, shrub, grass, flower that grows here? Does it make the greens greener? Or the golds more golden? Does knowing that this is a red maple and that a sugar maple matter? Must I have proof, with words and pictures from a book, that the blueberries that one spring magically covered the stony slope are dwarf sweet? Or, wait… are they low sweet? They are low, and they taste sweet and knowing what label botanists slapped on them will make them neither tall nor sour.

Yet every people everywhere have tried to order the living world. And people everywhere see the same basic order, because beneath the great variety in ordering and naming, there are deep underlying principles. Psychologists have found that some brain-damaged patients are unable to order and name living things; it turns out all have suffered damage in the same part of the brain. There must be a physical location where the ability to order and name the living world resides, scientists hypothesize, making this drive a function of being human.

The names, too, intrigue me. Sassafras, for instance. An unremarkable tree in every way, neither imposing nor flowery, "Joe the Plumber" of the arboreal world.

But now take its name. Sassafras. A tart and spicy word on the tongue, a combination of exotic sounds. Does it not raise the status of this humdrum tree several notches? It lifts it right out of the abyss of tawdry commonness and makes it memorable.

Take another name, an ugly one. Burdock. It so perfectly fits this alien with immense hairy leaves and roots that reach into the earth's bowels. Even when the name doesn't suit the plant at all, as in the case of vetch, an ugly name for a useful and delicate wildflower, I need to know it. Sassafras, burdock and vetch are the keys to simplifying this overwhelming green world.

The world turns on small events that add up to history. The plant world turns on small differences. The same flower with clusters of three or four or six or even seven tiny whorled leaves instead of eight is not the same flower at all. One is the fragrant bedstraw. The other the wild madder, an invasive that forms thick mats and chokes our native grasses.

In the woods I want to know each particular tree and its seasons, the blackberries and wood violets that grow underneath it, and the small desolate spaces left by forgotten trees that stood there once. To know all this, I need to know the tree from its neighbors. I need to pay attention to its bark, the edges of its leaves, the shape of its growth. Is it vase-like or spreading? Flat-topped or rounded? Is its bark smooth or warty, papery or plated? And the leaves. Opposite, compound, alternate, palmate, pinnately compound? And that's just their arrangements. Their shapes and edges merit a whole other lexicon.

I have learned a little. I proudly note that these young whips that have sprouted around the edges of the fields are poplars, not birches. Poplars, not aspens. This ability to detach a single tree from the green abundance is knowing the tree, and knowing the tree is integral to knowing the woods. It's a matter of divide and conquer.

"The real voyage of discovery consists not in seeking new landscapes but in having new eyes," Proust wrote.

In seeking new eyes I learn the pleasures of solitude, so different from loneliness. Engulfed in this rich benevolence, I am not alone. I wander in the shimmering grasses and blowzy flowers and saplings and am as serene as the trees that rise in the same small spot for decades, generating sustenance from their own shed leaves, a cycle of peace.

Will I know the world better by knowing this hill?

"The great revelation had never come," Virginia Woolf wrote. "Instead there were little daily miracles, illustrations, matches struck unexpectedly in the dark."

Loving the little daily miracles of a place is like loving a person. After the first flush of infatuation, a maturing follows, a deepening brought about through intimacy and understanding. It is that intimacy and understanding that I seek. Recognizing a plant among many others and knowing its name is like picking out a loved one from a hundred people walking away from a concert, knowing him by the tilt of the head, the swing of an arm.

If I can unravel this one small place into its strands I will begin to grasp it. Then each small venture, to the compost heap or the blueberry patch, or from the barn to the cabin will be a series of recognitions. Yes, I will nod. I know you. You with the velvety leaves reaching low, asking for my touch.

The Crickets Shall Sing

It started one February morning after our first idyllic summer in the cabin. A colossal machine, appropriately named brontosaurus, crawled up the hill and down to a distant corner. There it began to systematically chew up the dying apple trees. Its front-mounted arm rose like a monstrous elephant trunk sniffing the icy air, then came down on top of each tree, crushing it into rough chips that flew in all directions. The operator sat unmoving behind the wheel, creeping methodically down the rows, his face a mask of patient composure even as I stopped him several times a day, waving my arms in his path, to remind him to leave four rows around the perimeter untouched. That border would be a viable vestige of the former thousands, and with patience and labor perhaps yield decent fruit. And it would leave the large fields virtually treeless, a requirement for the ground nesting bird habitat we were creating.

A century ago, when agriculture reigned in Vermont, as in much of New England, some three-quarters of the state was grassland. As farmers left the rocky uplands for richer soil out west, forests sprang up where grass had been and ground-nesting birds lost much of their habitat. Today, as the ratio of field to forest continues to shrink, these birds are in dire need of unmowed grass in which to build nests and raise the next generations.

Our land, it turned out, is in a "Priority Block" for both the

Vermont Breeding Bird Atlas and the Vermont Butterfly Survey. So the U.S. Department of Agriculture offered a win-win deal. In return for keeping our acres as grassland, they would share the cost of clearing the orchard and for the next five summers, after the newborn birds had fledged, of cutting the fields.

Roy Pilcher, the local Audubon Society expert, has spent hours on our hill, crouching in grass, counting the growing population of birds and butterflies. On his first foray in the summer after the trees were cut, he found thirteen bird species, the most significant in terms of rarity being bobolinks and red-winged blackbirds. He also recorded five butterfly species, none rare but all beautiful. Subsequent field trips yielded more species, and each year the populations of existing species would grow. Five years after the trees were cleared, Roy counted thirty-two species.

But as the trees were being devoured, I didn't trust that any of this would happen. Within one week, at ten minutes per tree, the orchard lay in a wasteland of smashed tree parts. The devastation was horrifying. There, exposed, lay the land's injured ribs and welts, clefts and sockets, all its gashes laid open under the leaden sky.

True, the trees had not been the picture of health. They were diseased. Their bark was peeling. The promise wrapped in the buds sputtered briefly in frail blossoms that gave way to tiny leaves that were rolled and chomped by armies of invading insects. The fruit was as compromised as the leaves, sporting every disease known to apple trees. Their death cries rose through the overgrown, twisted branches. Yet one bite into the few edible ones among these ugly apples and a memory bloomed: the sharp, layered taste of how apples tasted before they were supersized and made to look perfect.

But now the ravage was complete. Decades of patient growth, of tenacious survival were spit out upon the denuded earth. Last summer's silky milkweed pods and thistle flowers, even the nettles lay mashed into the ground. All was flat, colorless, a sterile moonscape. The gray earth and suffocating sky, the desolation and cold were too much like the photos of Auschwitz years after liberation.

What had happened to the hardy seeds of grasses and flowers, to the wild strawberries and blueberries that lay dormant, waiting for the earth to warm? To the burrows of small animals, the mice, shrews and snakes that had lived in the tall grass for a hundred years? The brown rabbit that had once sat in front of our cabin, observing us silently, unafraid of these never-before-seen, large, giggling creatures? To the billions of unseen organisms that live in every cubic inch of earth? Even this hill in this harsh climate, so poor compared to the richness of a tropical rainforest, a hill that has known nothing but human management for generations, was a living sea of interdependent organisms. Scientists had hardly explored a fraction of this ecosystem's lives and understood little of its exquisite symbiosis – between trees, living fungus, dead trees, burrowing mammals and the universe of undiscovered insects in the soil. My brain couldn't even begin to grasp the atoms and the subatomic particles, the neutrinos and quarks that we can't see but that constitute all we can see, and which have been irreparably disturbed. What if, by cutting the trees, we had launched a chain of death that would spiral into extinction of this entire hill?

I knew I was vastly exaggerating the consequences, that guilt had robbed me of reason. I had studied and read enough to know better. The animals would wander back and the land would regenerate. Nature always yearns to return to its natural state. In this case, the natural state – at least until natural succession sets in – would be fields of grasses and wildflowers. Left alone, the empty chaos would grow into something beautiful. The orchard was not, after all, a natural landscape, having been planted and maintained by humans with their machinery and chemicals. Spring, followed by a rainy summer, would work their magic. The crickets and fireflies would move in, and butterflies would hover over the tall grasses. But looking around on that frigid February day it was hard to believe in anything good coming out of the flattened wasteland.

Winter

It was hard to believe in spring.

It's hard to believe in any season except the one I'm in. I'm always especially unprepared for winter, no matter how late it comes, as it did one year when each autumn day claimed to be *the* peak of blazing color, and even November retained more than a memory of splendor. And yet, I was still behind the seasons, so that when a cold rain dismantled the trees in a single night, I was incredulous.

"Only yesterday…" I kept repeating inanely.

That afternoon an hour of "mixed precipitation" formed a gleaming crust over the yellowing grass. I was struck by the bleakness. I believed when winter would come, it would be one of grand white flakes infusing the grayness with reflected light.

This powerful disconnect persists every year between my memories and reality. My eyes remain saturated with warmth and color. They have to adjust to appreciate winter's spare beauty.

In early winter, night swells into the afternoon and onto the late morning. When dawn finally comes, it's a dim, gray illumination. The sun barely edges above the circle of southern hills, and when it sets, it's no more than a pink sliver between the clouds and mountains. When the sliver winks out, darkness is complete.

During the night, an angry storm. Dry, hard, small flakes in intersecting lines, wind whipping them not into Van Gogh's fat swirls but into jagged bolts of lightning. When we wake, the windows are half buried.

By November, I begin the countdown to the winter solstice. The shortest day or the longest night. The earth is poised as far from the sun as it will be this whole year. By tomorrow, it will tilt ever so slightly toward the sun. Each day will then be a minute longer.

I make an effort to understand these events because I'm a creature of the day. Nocturnal people baffle me. Why miss out on daylight? Do they really prefer to spend their waking hours in artificial light? All spring and summer I rise with the sun and go to sleep with the dark. As the days shorten, I begin living in the future. Time, which has been scientifically shown to shrink as we age, expands. I count on the extra minute of light at the start and end of each day, an accumulation of minutes when the dark is held at bay.

The sun returns in late January, after a more or less continuous two-month absence. The nights also turn luminous. I stumble about after the sun sets, waiting for the moonrise. The Wolf Moon arrives during an icy spell. So named by Native Americans, it's closer to the earth than at any other time in the year, and so appears 14 percent larger. As it skirts the hump of Birdseye Mountain, the world goes silver. Each peak stands out sharply against the deep indigo sky. Silver shadows chase each other across the fields as the wind whips the snow into fantastic spires, mesas and hoodoos.

Resolute, every winter day I force myself to go outside. Today's air is alive with snow crystals. The Siberian cold insinuates itself between my mittens and sleeves. It enters my lungs and from there spreads through the organs, chilling from inside out. The wind rises from every surrounding valley. I stand alone, frail between the wind and infinity. I snap on skis and slide away.

A half dozen wild turkeys appear from beyond the trees. They strut past and disappear into the woods. These are followed by two white-tailed deer. They stop to look at me, and judging the distance safe, stay put. Not until I start skimming toward them do they move off, still at a regal pace, their tails loose. I climb to the cabin and stand against its eastern wall where Birdeye's icicles glimmer from its heights. A red fox trots into view. It stands still for a long time, its luxuriant tail quivering. Then it hops high several times, landing with its front legs in the snow. It lands and turns in circles, as if chasing its tail, and stands still once more, only to repeat the hopping. This odd dance is not for my benefit. It's listening for movement under snow and pouncing on the small animals it hears.

I ski toward the hedgerow where I'll be out of the wind. The snow is a blank canvas, and the night's events are writ large upon it. My skis float over the familiar small tracks. Then over a large four-padded one. A cat, very large, not the house variety. I don't want to guess. I move over tamped-down snow, a large deeryard where the animals had desperately dug for fallen apples, over yellow urine, and small, dark scat.

Everywhere are crisscrossing, meandering tracks. Standing in the middle of last night's tales, I decide to follow one, to see what the deer saw, to unravel the tangled yarn of their meanderings. They take me up the hill and back down, crossing other tracks. The tracks multiply in places, and in others rumple into unreadable snags. There is no way to know which were made by "my" deer. I cannot understand their movements. I remain enmeshed in my human web.

I refuse to think of winter as an endurance test. I will not escape to some warm place. So I told three neighbors. One, a transplant like us, noted that he and his wife will leave for Florida right after Christmas. I promised to leave footprints in their driveway after every snowstorm. Another, born here, complimented us on our endurance, but the glint in his eye spoke no admiration; he expected us to give up before too many more winters. Our elderly neighbors, whose history in these hills goes back generations, pursed their lips and nodded sagely. "Wait till the cold deadens your battery and freezes your clutch to the floor! Until the road down your hill is a tormented icescape! Oh, when the wind coats your windows with an inch of ice. You'll be searching for a deal on Carnival Cruise Lines!" Unformed words, held within unsmiling lips.

I wanted to explain that we want to stay the course. Because I want to be here to see the Wolf Moon rise, make sure the turkeys cross the field safely, hear the gnashing of boots on frozen snow, bask in the rare sunlight, and yes, feel the wind snatching at my throat.

Because how can I learn winter if I'm not here?

It's fairly easy to act the hero when venturing outside is a matter of choice and there's a warm house waiting upon return. It was harder, much harder, when we still lived in the cabin.

First, there was the trudge through the dark cold from the road, where we had to leave the car when there was snow. Carrying our stuff, including enough food for a few days, uphill some six hundred feet was enough to get the blood circulating, especially when it had to be repeated several times before everything was transported. Even more so when instead of soft snow, the ground was a treacherous tundra of repeatedly melted and frozen snow.

Then there was the cabin. So welcoming and homey in summer, it was a glaciated crypt when we arrived on winter nights. Ted was the fire master. I boiled water on the camp stove for tea, my hands shaking so that lighting a match was an achievement.

But within an hour, all was forgotten in the warmth swelling from the little stove, expanding in billowing circles until everything was saturated by luxurious heat, and the darkness banished by half a dozen candles. I could have sat up all night drinking tea or wine and watching that little iron box blaze away on apple branches.

Except I couldn't. Because drinking anything before sleep meant a night interrupted by multiple peeing trips outside. And even one such trip was to be avoided as long as possible and even a bit beyond.

First there was the matter of throwing on a bunch of clothes and shoes. We eliminated this step by learning to wrap the blankets around ourselves and slipping feet into boots that stood at a precise spot by the bed. Once out, I was blinded to the marvel of the starlit night, by the blast of wind that forced me to close my eyes. Groping half blind, I'd take a few steps gingerly, holding on to the side of the cabin. Then came the real test of mettle: exposing the lower half to the elements. The wind seemed to shift each time, suddenly blowing from the ground up in a perverse trick meant to chill me from inside in a matter of seconds. Getting back into the cabin provided instant relief, but getting back to sleep with frozen organs was not instantaneous.

Still, the discomforts were balanced by rewards. For the first time in our always busy lives, we could just hang out all day doing "nothing" but reading, napping, daydreaming, drinking bottles of red wine tempered with bars of dark chocolate, and indulging in very slow lovemaking.

Not so once our wonderful new house was completed with heated floors, sophisticated air exchange system, and steaming hot tub. In a house equipped with lights and hot water, there are things to do all day and before and after dinner too. It's the price of ease. And I'm not complaining.

A warm winter day today. I should enjoy it but don't. It feels uncomfortable and oddly menacing. It may be a normal aberration, but it's a reminder of the global changes even newcomers like us have noticed. Local nurseries selling plants for a zone or even two warmer than what used to be considered safe; a string of autumns with less than optimal color change due to too few cold nights; plants flowering earlier; eggplants and tomatoes ripening through mid October.

These personal observations are borne out by data gathered over the past four decades. The USDA's Agricultural Research Service is revising its 1990 plant hardiness zone map to reflect climate changes that are already underway. The growing season has increased by two weeks for frost-sensitive plants, and by three to four weeks for frost-hardy plants. The maple sugaring season starts seven days earlier on average and ends ten days sooner than it did forty years ago. Snow reflects sunlight, causing the temperature to drop, but with the first heavy snowfall arriving later, the cold arrives later too.

A recent report sponsored by the Union of Concerned Scientists predicts that between 2040 and 2069, Vermont's climate will shift to that of Pennsylvania's now. That will impact more than temperature.

One in four trees in Vermont's forests is a maple, providing, with birch and beech, the burst of reds, oranges and yellows that draw visitors from around the world. But the oaks and hickories, which predominate in warmer places like Pennsylvania and now account for less than 15 percent of the trees here, will overshadow the maples by the end of the century, the USDA Forest Service projects. The brilliance will be replaced by a blander brown.

These small events bring to mind the apocalyptic ones: ice caps melting, corals dying, animals shifting their range. Polar bears, frogs, bats, bees, butterflies demolished by strange diseases or disappearing habitat.

Still, when a warm day comes, I take advantage. I sweep out what used to be the storage shed for chemicals when this was a working orchard. A pair of barn swallows skim above me, outraged. They are the fortunate ones. The barn is the palace of winter bird habitats. Most birds pass the subzero nights in old nest cavities or under peeling bark or in vines covering buildings and under eaves. Purple finches roost en masse in pines and hemlocks. The titmice, chickadees, nuthatches and woodpeckers that frequent our birdfeeder use tree hollows. Turkeys and crows huddle in groups to pool their body heat. The ruffled grouse dig under snow or divebomb into a snowbank to dig a tunnel.

To keep their body temperature at the requisite 104 to 109 degrees, many birds grow a thicker coat of insulating feathers. They can also increase insulation by 50 percent simply by fluffing up their feathers and tucking in their necks, legs and wings, thus decreasing their surface area and heat loss. When none of these techniques suffices, birds do what we do: shiver to generate body heat. They have an additional advantage: a sophisticated heat exchange system that helps maintain their core temperature. As warm arterial blood is pumped toward the cold feet, it comes into close contact with the cooler blood returning through to the heart. This contact warms the returning blood so that it doesn't chill the body too much as it returns to the heart.

Insects, a lower life form, have some pretty sophisticated coping mechanisms as well. The caterpillar overwintering in the woodpile and the wooly bear curled up at the sunroom door produce chemicals that inhibit ice from forming in their tissues, permitting them to cool without freezing to temperatures as low as -56 degrees F. In other insects, freezing takes place in between cells but not within cells. Bees, metabolizing the honey and pollen collected over the summer, give off heat. Huddling in a ball that tightens as the temperature drops, they continue to generate heat.

Plants acclimate to subfreezing temperatures slowly, beginning in late summer, induced by decreasing day length. Acclimation involves a hormone that increases dramatically as daylight shrinks. It decreases the permeability of membranes to water, thus preventing water from entering and freezing in the cells. By fall, plants can withstand the first light frosts. Exposure to the first hard frost starts a second phase of acclimation, and the minimum survival temperature begins to decrease until the plant reaches its maximum resistance.

Trees not only survive the freeze but continue to function on many levels. When the ground is frozen but the temperature of the tree is above freezing, photosynthesis may continue in the bark and twigs, even when the bark is buried under snow. And the roots of some trees continue to absorb and conduct water through the tree even in frozen soil.

Today, the freeze is absolute. A major storm is making national news. I could sit by the window all day reading snow haiku. Tomorrow, I'll want to go outside, admire my tracks in the fresh snow, wear myself out traversing the hill. Tomorrow we'll have to reconnect ourselves to the world. But today I want to savor my good fortune.

"How're you surviving the winter?" concerned friends, convinced Vermont lies directly below the Arctic Circle, asked the first winter after our move.

"We have the best heating system in the world, so frostbite hasn't claimed any of our fingers or toes yet," I reassure them. But they ignore the sarcasm.

"But what about when you go out? Can you even get out, with all the snow..." they persist.

"Sure. We go out, every day. Although we usually wait for the daily blizzard to pass," I explain.

There's much I don't tell them. How I am breathless with gratitude for the collision of choice and luck that have brought us to this spot. Where I can work and walk and breathe in icy beauty. When more than half the world's population lives surrounded by steel and concrete, by light and noise, seeing only shards of sky, I sit here on top of the visible world.

The New Localism posits that people want community, which calls for physical closeness to others. I too enjoy coffee shops, farmers markets, libraries, biking trails and all kinds of community involvement, but my communal feelings stop at physical closeness. I'm happy to know that most people seek that closeness, and I sincerely wish them success in finding it. I feel a special benevolence toward my fellow humans, all seeking some measure of contentment, all battered by life. I especially feel this immense good will whenever I'm away from them.

And for an undeniably selfish reason. If they get what they need, I get to stay here, wrapped in silence and solitude.

Cabin Fever

I am lying with my ski-shod feet and upper arms out in the elements, the rest of me folded in snow. I had stopped flailing and yelling for help. The newly fallen, weightless snow is quicksand; the more I flail, the deeper I sink. And yelling, while not making things worse, is lost in the silence of the swaddling snow and the wind, which is blowing my hoarsening voice back into my hole.

Staring at the clouds skittering across the new moon, I hit my forehead with my hand, slowly stiffening in the thin glove. I'm not prone to dramatic physical gestures, but this demands one.

"Damn! Damn! Damn!" I shout once more into the night.

Any sane person would have taken up one of two offers for a night in a proper home, or gone to a motel. Normal people wouldn't have driven into a snowstorm after a day of skiing so they could sleep in a primitive cabin! I continue to rage silently, twisting my head and seeing only snow on every side.

Sleeping is at the moment a fantasy. First, we have to get to the cabin, perched at the top of the hill. Under normal circumstances, the climb is exhilarating. Tonight, circumstances are not normal. It's night, and the latest snowfall brings the total on the ground to about three feet. I estimate this by the depth to which my torso is buried and by the fact that I was able to climb over the gate, it being mostly under snow.

We were smart enough to remember to bring skis, knowing we'd need them to get to the cabin. Why not snowshoes? We don't have any. Nor headlamps either, which we do have but which are sitting on the headboard in the cabin. The real mystery is why Ted decided to *shovel* his way up. How does one shovel uphill, in the dark, in deep snow? Skis are the only way. The only reason I had not succeeded with them was that the snow was too soft, and once I fell, I was buried, as helpless as an upside down beetle. If only he had listened to me and used the skis, he could have pulled me out, and by now we'd both be in the cabin, building the fire.

In time, anger turns to worry. Is he buried too, somewhere above me? Would we both spend the night trapped in our separate holes? We would survive, maybe, but I am exhausted. From skiing or this struggle? Or from the early onset of hypothermia? Where could he be? Shoveling shouldn't have landed him in as deep a hole. You can't fall too far when shoveling, and without skis, he should be able to push himself out. He's fine, I tell myself. Still, irrational fears flare. Images of the young women forced into the ice-choked ocean as the liberating troops' fire was within earshot. Did they freeze or drown? Which came first?

Out of the darkness, booming, reverberating laughter. Ted is behind me, then in front of me. He drops the shovel, and stares at me, gesticulating, doubled over, practically foaming at the mouth with obscene hilarity, unable to speak.

It turns out he had not exactly shoveled a path, but had tamped the snow down and then cut steps into it. He pulls me out, still guffawing, ignoring my rage. We walk to the cabin, upright all the way. He drags my skis and both our bags. It's the least he can do and hardly enough. I continue to shed fury like fallen scales, until we drop into bed, sans the hot bath.

Why did two rational, mature people choose to do such a blatantly stupid thing as to struggle up to an unheated cabin at night in deep snow? Because we were feverishly in love with that little cabin on the hilltop.

The cabin provided what a house could not. I am convinced that every "adventure travel" company would promptly go out of business, and video games would vanish if more people had primitive cabins. Living without electricity and running water, without central heat and a driveway to the door provides plenty of challenges. And challenges have a way of turning into adventures, which have to be overcome through creativity and hard-won wisdom, providing thrills several rungs above the fabricated ones we pay for.

So I tried to explain to the many skeptics who questioned the lack of running water and electricity. Electricity? Who needs it? Electricity means a vacuum cleaner. A broom, I insisted, is far superior, providing a meditative Zen experience. Plumbing? Yes, an indoor toilet might be nice on winter nights, but who wants to do dishes?

It was a fine dwelling without the responsibilities of a house, a perfect retreat without the liabilities of a second home. It was, more than anything, a living demonstration of just how little we need to be content. A poster I created and framed said it all: "Show me what's missing from this cabin and I'll show you how to be happy without it." Of the very few friends who visited, none ever showed any interest in the poster's wisdom.

Indeed, one of the cabin's chief charms was the very fact that we had few visitors. Those ready to brave a night in the cabin were as enthusiastic as we were about its primitive allure. They were interested in the engineering marvels of the marine toilet, and enjoyed the toast I scorched on the flame of the camping stove. They were helpful in small ways; collecting wood for the fire pit where we grilled entire dinners, picking apples for hours, and inquiring about the wildflowers' names.

In fact, except for our children, only three friends visited over four years, and no one ever took us up on an invitation for a winter getaway. They mumbled protests about having to step out at night to pee, and about showers, challenges that we had long before overcome with simple solutions.

In summer, two sun showers consisting of transparent plastic bags were laid on the grass. By late afternoon on sunny days, the contents would reach scorching temperatures and would have to be diluted with cold water. In winter, we placed a round metal tub designed to water cattle in front of the stove. Two kettles of hot water filled the tub a third of the way, enough to reach my waist if I could maneuver my legs into a tight cross-legged position. Unable to move once in position, I would sit there as the water cooled and I slowly turned into a paraplegic. Then I would beg Ted to lift me out, an occasion he never failed to use to teach me the lesson I refused to learn. He was, I insisted, simply jealous, since he had to squat while I poured water over him. Whoever said size was an advantage?

I described to friends the wonder of being outside on a winter night, an experience that could not be avoided by anyone over a certain age sleeping in the cabin.

"Imagine a still moonless night, with a billion stars piercing the black sky," I would begin, only to be met with silly questions about wild animals. Even the bulls and cows were gone. For good.

In truth, coyotes did prowl around, sometimes too close for comfort. Their yowls pierced the silence much more vehemently than the stars ever pierced the sky. I learned to take only a few steps from the porch, varying the direction so as not to pollute any one spot.

More bothersome were the mosquitoes. Much of the time, our windy hilltop enjoys mosquito-free evenings. But on rare nights, when the wind ceases and the humidity rises, the mosquitoes become so numerous they form a wavering, sinister curtain. The quickest trip outdoors to pee can result in multiple bites in sensitive areas.

All these dangers paled in the face of our chief friend and foe: the wind. Gusts of forty mph in the village gather force, adding twenty or more miles as they rise. Three times the cabin was moved by such gales, each time shifting a couple of feet westward, shoved by a Nor'easter. Miraculously, except for a couple of shattered picture frames and spilled coffee grounds, it survived unscathed each time. More miraculously, we were never present, saving us from Dorothean terrors.

A professional team secured the cabin after the second move, pouring a foundation and bolting it down with metal chains. The wind, undeterred, wrenched the bolts out of the frozen earth, flinging them like spent trophies in the snow. Only the metal bathtub, halfway under the cabin and filled with rainwater frozen solid, kept the cabin from sliding right off the cement foundation. The professionals returned, regarded the cabin silently and left. They came back with bigger bolts that they drove into the foundation and thicker chains to secure the cabin to the bolts. That was last year. The cabin is still in place. But having witnessed the wind's violence on large healthy trees, on newly laid roofs, on planks torn from picnic tables and blown across tall fences, on crumpled barns and splintered outbuildings, we have no illusions.

For now, the cabin continues to live on the highest point on the hill, looking down at the house and barn, the three buildings that form our compound. It's where I come in the morning to work. Its brave little chimney, pointing into the wild air, is the last sight I see from bed at night.

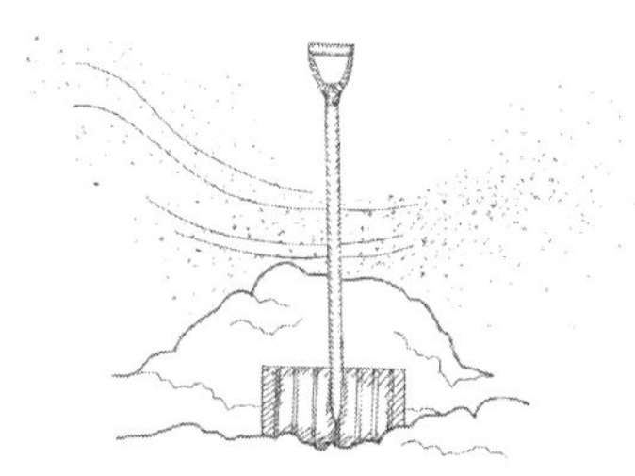

Snow

Even in late winter, when I should know better, Jeff's truck at the bottom of the driveway brings joy, a sound filled with the promise of deliverance. With his big machine and plow mounted at a rakish angle, Jeff will make short order of the heavy layers that fell, drifted and cascaded all day and night on our driveway.

When he leaves, his job is done, and done well. The road curves sinuously, a sharp canyon between steep snow walls. We come out and walk up and down just for the pleasure of walking with such ease, observing the layers of snow, ice and sand in the canyon walls, as fluid and beautiful as an oil abstract. It's wonderful, as the wind picks up above us, to be in this protected narrow world.

The wind of course, is the beginning of the end of Jeff's handiwork.

"You know what we'll be faced with tomorrow," Ted remarks sagely as we complete the survey.

"Maybe it'll blow from the east and then there'll be nothing to blow since the town road is all clear," I answer, the positive lilt in my voice sounding false even to me.

"You know it never blows from there," Ted points out, which is something I've had time to observe. It blows from the northwest or southwest, and when it's a nor'easter, from the south. Never from the east. And from any of these directions, wind on snow-covered fields is bad news.

Next morning, we can see that the southern field is denuded. Stiff pockets of grass are showing through the thin cover. We can also see that the driveway is no longer visible. The snow that covered acres of fields is now settled across the driveway in uneven heaps, low piles and monstrous masses. Not enough to justify calling Jeff again. We can handle it.

We pile on the layers and pick up our implement of choice. My snow shovel is a smaller than standard version, fire engine red, with an ergonomic bent to the handle that's meant to eliminate the backache that follows the lifting and heaving of a couple of tons of snow. Dragging the shovels, we step into what the thermometer assured us was a balmy twenty-one degrees, warm enough for cold-hardened Vermonters like us to require only woolen gloves and a shell.

Surveying the damage, we fall into our individual default modes.

"It's not too bad," I venture, looking at the malevolent drifts. "We can just dig two paths for the tires along the curvy sections."

"That'll only help going down," Ted points out. "We need to move enough snow to allow for skidding."

"If we dig sharp paths for the tires we won't skid," I insist.

"You're so wrong. What about…" but I'm walking away, dragging my ergonomic shovel, and miss the list of dire possibilities.

Ted works up an enviable rhythm, his eyes narrowing into slits of focused concentration. On the other hand, it may just be a semi catatonic state that he enters by mid-February when shoveling. Push, raise, fling, push, raise, fling. He wastes no words on convincing the likes of me of his superior snow-judging powers.

I dig in and after a few shovelfuls decide to try a different angle. Perhaps if I dig in from the side… or fling over my head rather than twisting each time. Maybe I should section the accumulation into even amounts first. Then again, that's an extra and probably wasted step. So I start a tire-sized row, walk ten feet and start in the other direction. Now

I can see a beginning and an end. The issue is the middle.

It's the snow, I finally decide. What was pure powder, marvelous fluff, has become tonnage. How has it happened? Why would the snow quadruple its weight overnight? It must be perception, surely not fact. But then, as I recently learned, in this case perception and fact just happen to merge seamlessly.

New fallen snow undergoes very rapid change as crystals are transformed into aggregates of ice grains. Within hours, snow density may double. This is followed by settling, in this case aided by wind, which reduces the spaces between the snow grains further and increases its density.

I ponder these mysteries as I move between the leaden packs. Ted is moving faster than me, so we meet not quite in the middle.

"Not a bad day's work," I offer. "More productive and less boring than lifting weights in some health club."

He yells something contrary moving uphill. But his words are carried off, sucked into the maw of the whipping air.

A First-World Habitat

The decision to build a house ahead of schedule was made one night in the cabin in the dead of winter, precipitated by a final impasse on potty issues.

It had been hovering at around five degrees for two nights. Ted had been heroically keeping the fire going, rising to feed the stove while I rose to peek above the blankets, note that it was still dark and slide back down. Toward early morning, when it became unbearable, I wrapped myself in all the blankets, slid my feet into boots, and dragged myself out to pee.

On the third night, as the temperature and winds showed no inclination to relent, Ted decided the time was ripe to carry out his long-delayed threat.

Without a word, he brought in the dreaded pail. Then, ignoring my accusing looks, sat down on the daybed to read, the miner's lamp on his forehead glinting evilly.

But he couldn't not hear me. I launched into well-reasoned, then anguished entreaties, and finally whining pleas.

"Fuhgeddaboutit," he growled in response.

So began the saga of what would come to be known as "The Building." And of our huge learning curve, as we discovered just how incredibly ill equipped we were to undertake such a monumental project due to total lack of talent, experience and interest, which resulted in ignorance so deep that for a long time we were clueless about how much we didn't know.

The most complex building job we had ever tackled was having new kitchen cabinets and countertops installed. That was the sum total of our combined expertise. Add to this the fact that we both disliked working on anything that had to do with maintenance, from touch-up painting to replacing a torn screen; that we would have chosen to go without meals rather than become do-it-yourselfers on even the simplest tasks; and that we had spent our lives admiring the landscape around houses, ignoring the houses themselves; that therefore we had no awareness of architecture in any form; and that we were ignorant of the existence of numerous television programs devoted solely to home improvement, watched by millions who would never be involved in more than a bathroom remodeling.

And here we were, planning a whole house! Where no house had ever existed. And not just any house; a "green" house on a wind-scoured, rain-lashed hilltop; a house that will need a foundation dug, a long driveway carved, and a new well blasted through rock. That will call for electricity, which will have to be dragged up and trenched through hundreds of feet, a vast system to dispose of waste, and massive reinforcement against the infamous winds.

Where, how does one begin?

Since almost everything I learned in life I learned from books, I bought a few. These tomes were the beginning of my new life, a life that outside of work and family obligations was devoted to "The Building."

First, my unquenchable thirst for reading was put on indefinite hold. Radio news supplanted newspapers. Books and magazines became limited to those that related to building, architecture and design. After the first few weeks, we learned enough to split up the monumental task. Ted was responsible for becoming informed about the intricacies of construction, covering such arcane topics as heating systems including solar, wind and geothermal options, foundations and insulation, roofing materials and the endless choices in windows. He spent nights working out lengthy formulas to determine the cost vs. efficiency of these systems. I, meanwhile, was discovering that "old" and "modern" were not the only two architectural options.

The inflow of all this novel information created a state of helpless confusion, our minds flooded with so much esoteric, complex, often conflicting, always amazing data. Who, living in a built house, knows about the complexities of plumbing systems? Or the spacing of studs? And the R-values of insulation? Who ever questions where the flushed water goes? Who even cares? Surely, we didn't. But now that our future lives and our savings were on the line, the brilliance of a house's innards became the subject of animated conversation.

The "organic" design phase lasted several months. The geodesic dome had a relatively short lifespan, having been discarded as an architectural foible decades before. An earth shelter? Having half the house buried underground didn't fit in with my dream of a mostly glass house. The cozy feeling promised by a round pedestal house was intriguing. Elevated, leaving barely a footprint, this option occupied us for several weeks. Then, seeing that none existed in all of New England, or at least none that were happily occupied, that too was abandoned. So were the various permutations of earth-based buildings. Earthbag, rammed, corncob and bale houses could all have serious mold problems with the wind driven-rain on our hill.

The nail that sealed the fate of all of these unconventional houses was learning that they were built mostly through the owners' sweat equity, with assistance from many semi-professional friends. We had spent our lives pursuing ends that at no point intersected with any of the practical skills required to make sweat equity useful. Our friends were, like us, professionals who moved into previously built and occupied houses, some of which were apartments with superintendents who took care of the least repair. It very quickly became evident that every inch of our house would have to be built by professionals.

As it turned out, that was the wisest decision we made during the entire enterprise.

By early the following spring, we felt we had learned enough to ask dumb questions. It was time to find an architect who would be responsive to our dreams and our pocketbook. Asking but getting no personal recommendations, we embarked on a search through the Internet, local newspapers, and architectural and construction magazines.

An established architect with a large office showed us a series of efficient but uninspired houses. Another one came with a self-described "solid reputation" and an astronomical estimate. An "innovative," young architect fit our requirements and budget. Sadly, this would be his very first project since leaving a company that refused to let him "fly solo." We were leery of having him try out his wings on us. An architect in a nearby town had experience building elegant and huge "green" houses, a screaming oxymoron I was prepared to ignore. But he was taking off for an extended journey to each of the world's rain forests, with no specific return date.

Tim was the first in a long series of compromises. Pleasant, enthusiastic, and possessing a decent record, he was "extremely interested" in green design, and was "extremely excited" about learning on the job by doing extensive research and relying on other professionals such as engineers and solar experts. He suggested bringing a contractor on board early to ensure that his design was in line with our budget. And he was willing to provide less than a full range of shockingly costly services.

Tim seemed almost as thrilled about our house and as interested in every detail as we were rapidly becoming. He drove to our hill numerous times under various weather conditions. He bounded about for entire afternoons, his variously colored caps appearing unexpectedly from every direction, looking for the perfect site, which we had picked out the first time we stood on the hill. Ultimately, closing in on the very same spot slightly below the top of the hill, he recommended a long list of consultants who would precede what I considered the fun part, where we got to pick out the style and the number and size of rooms.

First was the site designer who would develop a site plan with a contour map, design the driveway and the septic system. Then more "pre-design" information was required and several more consultants had to be lined up and paid: a solar expert, a geothermal expert, a structural engineer. The local power provider to determine how feasible (read: costly) extending power to the hilltop and burying the cable would be. An excavator to do test pits for the foundation and the septic, who couldn't come until the roads dried out. And who, after finally arriving to do the test pits, very logically forewarned that he had no way of knowing what lay under what seemed like soft ledge without blasting through the actual rock face.

We were now a couple of months behind schedule for an early fall start and still ignorant about architectural options. I was happily completing the "thought list" Tim had given me, which so far was the only aspect I understood thoroughly. Yes, I wanted high ceilings, I noted on the questionnaire. Also a large kitchen, a good-sized pantry, and of course, glass throughout. And wood floors and a huge, round sunroom with a vaulted ceiling. The bedrooms could be modestly sized, but a large entrance hall was a must after three decades with a hall too small for two people to stand within acceptable personal space. And yes, I did really like large bathrooms. In the additional information section I noted that a sunken garden would be perfect between the house and garage, as would a sinuous dry stone wall at the bottom of the rise. One not quite as elaborate as Andy Goldworthy's mile-long masterpiece at Storm King Sculpture Garden in New York. A more modest derivative.

Ted's must-haves were fewer. He insisted on an attached garage, incomprehensibly rare in cold Vermont, putting an end to the sunken garden. He also requested an elaborate wood-burning Russian stove, which with its tremendous mass and clever recirculation pipes would heat the entire house.

All the learning and architectural searching took up three seasons. We'd have to wait for spring to start. We were behind. But enormously proud of our newfound knowledge. Ready to participate in designing the actual house. And gaining confidence in the thrilling spring that awaited us.

Groundhog

Did the groundhog see its shadow? I'm likely the only person in these United States who doesn't have the answer to this simple yes/no question. That's because I wouldn't care even if this bizarre ritual were based on the best science. Because I know, better than any rodent. That although two days ago an errant storm laid another foot of snow on top of the crusty foot already laying siege to the fields. That despite nights that dip into the single digits. And the trucks still crisscrossing frozen Lake Bomoseen. That all these are merely circumstantial evidence. The truth is, this winter is rapidly pulling up his robes, gathering his icy breath, snapping off his signature icicles and retreating to the tops of the Greens and the Adirondacks, where he'll lie, shrinking daily upward toward the treeline until only the Three Sisters will glimmer white in spring's aquamarine sky.

The facts are these: the nights are shrinking, the dark is retreating, light rules the world longer each day. By the end of this final week of February, the sun will rise ten minutes earlier and set ten minutes later than the previous week, slashing a full twenty minutes off the dark and handing it to the strengthening day.

The sun rises not only earlier but a good deal higher. No longer languishing behind the flank of Birdseye, it now muscles its way up swiftly from the mountain's hollow. A cool white disc for months, a promise unfulfilled, it's suddenly providing real heat again.

These days I find myself intrigued less by the long, exposed views of winter and more by the changing quality of light. I search for the Northern Lights in vain, that phenomenon that draws shimmering curtains of color across the night sky as winter wears thin.

But these are, after all, heavenly phenomena, fine for us to observe but hardly meaningful when life on earth is an unbroken white. Aha, but yesterday, the sun forced its way through the shell I was wearing, heating the skin on my back, and landing the melting snow off the highest branches with a syncopated melody of drops. It hit me with shards of light through the trunks, making its intentions clear. And the sap has surely begun to surge through the sugar maples because some intrepid farmers have already hung out a few tentative buckets.

Yesterday afternoon a groundhog circled the cabin, blindly poking his snout into the foundation, his stiff tail dragging uselessly behind. Why did it leave its safe hole to wander around the jarring light and cold? Perhaps it too sensed the change, and came looking for a convenient garden to invade. I have no idea whether or not it saw its shadow.

There will no doubt be more snow. But looking through these narrow windows between seasons I see spring gathering its countless small forces for its immense green gush.

First week of April, and the tops of the trees in the hedgerow are tinged with the red of unfurling buds. The earth is releasing its winter dampness and with it, pushing up the first tentative blades of grass. They are as green and tough as before, but sparser.

A month later, the large wood chips that had been the apple trees are invisible, swiftly disintegrating into new soil to feed the riotous growth. The empty spots where the vegetation had been crushed sports mats of intensely blue veronica. The other fifteen species of wildflowers I had counted the previous July are back. The greater the destruction, the more flowers. In some places, the fields look like cultivated wildflower gardens.

I am ecstatic in the green expanse, grateful to be forgiven for the violation we had perpetrated. I vow to never destroy anything on our land again, to be the guardian I always meant to be.

Mostly, though, I am awed. All of nature's regenerative power seems to have been concentrated right here, pent up into a tight network of thrusting roots, of seeds packed with life, of stems pulsating with growth, released on this hill to rage in flowering splendor.

More grateful than I could ever be are the birds and bees and butterflies and the millions of insects unseen and unloved that crawl, fly, slither and hop on and below the earth.

I wander dreamily through the fields. Swallowtails and monarch butterflies float on the warm currents of air that snake into my body. Lording it over everything are the birds, whose sheer numbers and powerful life force had turned the fields into a throbbing, noisy nursery.

In *The Road*, a chilling dystopian novel by Cormac McCarthy, the earth is a wasteland. The only sound in this dead world is the wind, howling through the skeletons of trees. The most painful absence is the sound of birds. The total desolation of that absence is horrifying.

"Start praying to birds in ecstasy! Cherish this ecstasy, however senseless it may seem to people," Father Zosima tells Alyosha in *The Brothers Karamazov*.

And I do, I do.

One spring day, spotting a hated mustard growing tall in the distance, I rush over and bend to yank it out. And find myself looking down into a craftily constructed little nest. Four pairs of tiny eyes look back at me. Four pinpoints of unblinking, focused light. Minutes pass while the birds and I observe each other silently.

What do they see? Much more than I see.

Birds' vision is sharper and they can see greater distances than humans can. More impressively, birds can see colors in the ultraviolet range that is invisible to the human eye. It's as hard for us to imagine how birds perceive color as it is for a colorblind person to imagine full-color vision. Do they see me in a glowing purple haze? Or in bands of orange?

So those miniscule eyes can see more, but I have the advantage of language. I feel that I should talk to these birds as I would to an infant, in a warm, sing-song voice. I should let them know that I present no danger, that I am just admiring their luminous eyes, that I wish I could hold them. But I can think of nothing to say that would interest them.

So I just watch, barely breathing. The birds are dark and tiny and intense. Soon, they will rise in wobbly flight, flit over the grass, and speckle the air with bounced sun in an ecstasy of freedom. And I, earthbound, will admire.

I am thinking all this, lost in this silent, cross-species examination. Suddenly, all four tiny beaks open in unison and out of them erupts a high-pitched, ear-splitting screech. The sound pierces my clothes and goes straight to my heart. I stagger backwards. Whatever had been was over. I am now the intruder.

I retreat indoors and stay there the rest of the day, staring through the windows.

Reading for Shapes

Back in New York at work, the cabin abandoned except for weekends, we're still pursuing the research phase of The Building, I barely have time to notice that by mid-March the grass in Central Park's Sheep Meadow is showing a rush of green. I have homework to do.

Once, very recently in fact, architecture was like a subtle spice in a well-prepared dish; an important ingredient, necessary even, but not directly noticed. What mattered was the food surrounding the spice, or in my case, the landscape surrounding the house.

Even in midtown Manhattan, home to the globe's most recognizable skyline, I rarely glanced upward to admire the buildings that made up that famous skyline. I was as oblivious to the exotic turrets and elegant columns as to the stunning glass facades and ziggurat hanging gardens. When One57, rising a thousand feet above Central Park, was being constructed a couple of blocks from my office, I walked right by it repeatedly, my eyes focused on the flowering trees in the park, ignoring the unique bent glass facade that appeared on every tourist's list. I knew the columnar front of the Metropolitan Museum and the massive stones of the Museum of Natural History. The brownstones on either side of Central Park were interesting, but more interesting was the park they flanked, where the theater and skating rink and other famous structures were merely an interruption of the cherished sea of green.

This age of architectural innocence came to an abrupt end when

The Building age began. After months of immersion, I was like a person blind from birth who is miraculously given the gift of sight. And like such people, I was suddenly overcome by all I had been missing, wild-eyed with the shock of the new and the beautiful. There was art all around me! Not just in the famous fronts and multifarious tops of skyscrapers but in virtually every window frame and doorway, every lobby and storefront. It was inundating, staggering, exhausting. It compounded Manhattan's already crushing weight on frayed nerves. The walk between Grand Central Station and my office, or my office and the subway stop two blocks away, turned into a frenzy of agitated staring.

After Manhattan's distracting demands for attention, driving around Vermont and observing one house at a time was a soothing reprieve. The Greek revival farmhouses with their elegant proportions were my favorite. Ted liked the stately Colonials that lined the village squares. We both admired the large, airy barn-like houses. Ski-lodges were an excellent model, as were the elaborate log cabins and the few beautiful Craftsman bungalows. We both disliked the overused prow-styles and the McMansions that had recently sprouted around Manchester in southern Vermont.

We were free to choose any style from any era – and that was precisely the problem. As the proverbial wandering Jews, we had no connection -- historical, familial, aesthetic – to architectural history. Our parents had lived mostly in apartments. Our grandparents had spent their days in dark, squalid spaces on narrow city streets or along muddy roads in Eastern European villages. From the house in Cluj where I had spent part of my childhood I remembered only the damp, overgrown garden, the hanging shrubbery below the chestnut trees. Ted, born in a small town in Hungary, vaguely remembered a yellow box with many windows; his only clear recollection was the river that flowed where the yard ended. The houses were not important to our families, and therefore barely remembered by us. Jews, after millennia of persecution, didn't get attached to anything that couldn't move with them. Our past was a gaping blank. We had nothing to hark back to.

Such unfettered freedom was paralyzing. We liked almost everything, and yet didn't like anything quite enough. None seemed right on our wide open hill. Eventually, we came up with an explanation we accepted due to the lack of a better one. All the houses we liked and all the ones we didn't had one thing in common: a front and a back. They were designed to front a street. On our hill, there would be no front and back; the house would be visible and the views spectacular from all sides. Therefore, every side, even the roof, would have equal importance.

Leafing through a gorgeous book on Japanese gardens, it struck me. A Japanese style house! A cube rather than a rectangle, a low, sprawling structure rather than a steep one. I was taken with the simplicity and serenity of Japanese architecture.

But who would design such a house? Surely not our architect, a native Vermonter steeped in the local vernacular, who didn't even posses a passport. And who would build such a house? Local builders' Websites featured the very houses the architect would design.

Then, in the midst of an unfocused search, as if summoned by magic, "Haiku Houses" appeared on my screen.

Here was an American company fully engaged in designing "country houses of 16th Century Japan." They were linked to a past defined by "high culture and great respect for nature and beauty." Their spaciousness "invited nature into the house," and even the sun was "invited into the heart of the home." They were constructed of various woods and impressive Douglas fir poles, giving a feeling of "living among the trees in the forest."

I sighed with wonder. I was immensely grateful – to the Internet, to American entrepreneurial spirit, to the Japanese aesthetic.

Ted received the link to the site immediately, but there was no immediate sharing of my unbounded excitement. By the time I got home he had looked briefly, he reported.

"And? Can you believe they exist?"

"Sure, why not? It's a big country, everything exists here."

"Well, okay, but isn't it incredible that we found it?"

"You found it," he corrected, as if that had anything to do with the sheer marvel of it.

"A Haiku house! It's so perfect! Exactly what we were searching for!"

"I'm not sure that's what we were searching for," he opined in measured tones. I looked at him, trying to process what my ears heard. Slowly, his lack of enthusiasm began to penetrate my shocked brain.

"You mean you don't like them? How could you not? They're simply *the* most beautiful structures and absolutely perfect for the hill."

Ted liked them all right. On paper, he said. And if he saw them in real life in Japan or even in San Francisco, where he thought he might have seen some, he would probably like them very much. But not in Vermont.

Astonished, I denounced his lack of imagination and sense of adventure, to which he took great exception, hurling a long string of adjectives to justify his position. "Incongruous, out of place, weird, strange." These degenerated into "grotesque" and finally, "stupid."

I stood my ground. I left strategically placed books around the house. Photos and drawings appeared on the refrigerator door. Emails were sent, opened and not responded to. Days passed with little conversation. One more lengthy argument, and right or wrong, it became clear that there would be no "Haiku House" on our Vermont hill.

Undaunted by this failure to convince Ted of my infallible architectural sophistication, I moved on.

Neighbors lent me a book by Sarah Susanke, a Midwestern architect. As its title suggests, *House Not So Big* espoused small houses in which each square foot was designed to fit a specific aspect of one's lifestyle. Initially, the exteriors grabbed my attention. Here were square, low-slung houses, a common style all over the Midwest that I had never noticed in my blind-to-architecture days. This led to a series of books on Frank Lloyd Wright's designs. I even read his biography, learning to dislike the man but admire his work.

It all made perfect sense. Wright's houses were designed for the prairie. Our property was in fact an open, tall-grass prairie on a rounded hill. It begged for just that kind of low slung, hip-roofed house in muted earth tones, a house organic to the landscape, echoing the hills that surround it. Its modest size would be in keeping with our wish to make the smallest possible footprint on the land. Its cube shape and low, spreading roof were even somewhat reminiscent of Japanese architecture. And while different from typical Vermont houses, it would not appear out of place. Ted and I were once again in harmonious agreement.

The architect, meanwhile, having no knowledge of the long road we had traveled to arrive at our fortunate discovery, looked uncharacteristically unexcited when we shared our wish for a prairie house, a Frank Lloyd Wright derivative. To his credit, he didn't dismiss it out of hand. It was simply not a style he had ever worked with. Then, revving up his enthusiasm a couple of notches until it almost reached its customary level, he assured us that he was eager to learn more. We left him with photos and drawings, and pointed out the one closest to our ideal.

A couple of weeks later, the drawings were complete. We arrived at Tim's office ready to be shocked into admiration at the seamless application of our vision to paper. The house he designed was indeed pretty, but baffling. Where did those four dormers come from? And why were the bedrooms upstairs when we said no second floor? What about that garage? Does a breezeway on a January night really attach the garage to the house or is it a recipe for an arctic wind tunnel?

We explained that his design was indeed a lovely Vermont cape, but not the house we had asked for. If we had wanted this kind of house, we could have bought plans off the shelf. What we wanted didn't exist on the shelf, which was why we hired him.

Tim took it well. The next time we met, the design vaguely reflected our vision. Each subsequent meeting brought it incrementally closer. Sometimes the increments were barely perceptible, but over time, the house, now a simple cube with banks of tall windows, was close enough so we could start dividing the space into rooms.

Over the next two months, each room was shrunk several times, culminating in a 42- by 42-foot footprint, just large enough to provide a sense of space. The vaulted circular sunroom devolved into a small screened porch. The guest rooms were shrunk to the width of a bed and night tables. The bedroom was moved to a second floor with half its height sunken into the living room, retaining the low-to-the-ground look while eliminating the too sprawling feel that threatened the design. Within the 2,100 square feet, the architect fit a roomy kitchen and large entrance and an upstairs landing that would serve as Ted's office. The wall in this landing was moved three times in an effort to expand the width to six feet, the minimum for a guest bed. Every inch added to the landing was an inch deducted from the stairs. This, we finally understood, was how one created a small footprint. The living room appeared large thanks to the all-glass south-facing wall and nine-to fourteen-foot ceilings. The architect assured us that anyone could build it, and do it for well under $150 a square foot.

We left with four large drawings showing the floor and framing plans, the sections, and the elevations, with a woman – presumably me -- climbing the stairs.

We were so close.

Spring

By then it was May, and the spring that was about to happen was here. Arriving at the cabin one evening, we open the car door and the song of a thousand peepers from the pond across the road pours in. The starkness of mud season had given way to a riot of throbbing life.

I wake long before the sun begins to tint the sky and listen. A lone robin breaks the air with its sharp song. The sound nears, until it seems the bird is perched outside the window. Another joins, then both leave and silence settles once more. I drift off, and when I wake again, the sky is filled with bright violet stripes. Within minutes, the sun heralds the day with a wild surge.

Birds soar and sing as if there had never been a sunrise before, as if this day is the first and the last. The young poplars filling in where the apple trees were felled are whippy with new life. The mountains radiate the deep burgundy of bulging maple buds. The nearby low hills sport new leaves in every shade of green ever known and many yet unnamed. Whoever believes fall is the only season of stunning foliage has not seen spring in Vermont. A truth.

Honeybees swarm the dandelions, the wild strawberries, the forget-me-nots and violets. A walk under the flowering apple trees is a walk in a beehive. The grass is a wilderness of shoots, stems, leaves, drinking sunlight, rain, air. As thick and glossy as an animal's pelt, it gives the lie to the dullness of watching grass grow. It has a will of its own. Untilled, unweeded, unmanaged, crawling with huge iridescent beetles, with snakes and voles. It's powerful, unmanageable, disorderly, the antithesis of an antiseptic, pesticided, herbicided lawn.

Most dazzling and most shameless are the flowers. Even these meek spring blooms are sexual. Summer's flowers, the brilliant Black-eyed-Susan, the shockingly pink thistle, even the modest white yarrow are blatantly sensual. They literally live for sex. A flower is, in fact, a sex organ with an ovary and with a male stamen with pollen, which needs to get into the ovary to fertilize the ovule. For this, help is needed. So flowers enlist pollinators that fly, crawl and walk. They seduce them with colors, brilliant to us and even more so to animals, who see colors through the ultraviolet range that's invisible to us.

Demure white and cream flowers stand out as much as the loud ones, but they do so in the dark, attracting bats and shrews. Some, like our wild roses and iris, even offer landing strips on their petals, inviting tired insects to take a break.

Warmth is another tool flowers use. The unloved skunk cabbage that you see in any damp New England area in early spring stays between fifty-nine and seventy-two degrees for two weeks in February and March, sitting in a ring of melting snow. Philodendron plants in Brazil maintain a temperature of one hundred and fifteen degrees in fifty-degree temperature. To insects with a desire for warmth, these plants are irresistible.

Their intoxicating or sickening aromas also beguile insects. Some flowers smell like food to their pollinators. That's how the venus flytrap lures insects into its ingenious trap. Others smell like the sex pheromones of insects or like excrement or like a rotting corpse. Insects revel in the carrion odor of black cohosh, which in late summer light up Northeast forests with their white spikes.

Nectar, the sugary liquid glistening in the bottom of an open flower, is as irresistible to animals as fine chocolate to us. If that's not incentive enough, flowers spike it up -- nectar has recently been found to contain a jolt of caffeine and a touch of nicotine. We don't know if bees get a buzz, but experiments show they prefer the caffeinated version.

Some liaisons can be deadly. One orchid attaches its pollinium – lumps of coagulated pollen -- to the eye of the moth that pollinates it. Others attach the pollinium to the tongues of birds, preventing them from eating. Our New England flowers use more mundane murder weapons. Gnats that enter jack-in-the-pulpit can escape if they enter a male flower, but are trapped and die in female flowers.

Walking through the fields late in the season, I become covered with clinging burrs and sticky seeds; I too have been recruited to carry seeds of thistle, bedstraw or clover. I pick them off, but what about the furry voles and rabbits. And imagine the porcupines!

Not all flowers are femmes fatale. Grasses and most trees bear inconspicuous blossoms that depend on the wind rather than animals. This saves the plants the enormous energy needed to put on a showy display and generate complicated aromas. Instead, they produce astounding numbers of seeds to ensure that a few are blown to an optimal spot.

But I prefer the blousy beauties around me as I plod toward the still pale blackberries, hoping for a few that have surged ahead of schedule.

In the expanding light and warmth, life is a riot of irrepressible gusto, of flowering, leafing, wriggling, budding, of energy suffusing birds, bees, plants, and me too. Indoors, I am filled with anxiety for all that I'm missing out there. Outdoors, bending to the young birches, I raise my head when the hawk's shadow passes over and realize I've missed the scattering of the ethereal apple petals. And when did the swallow move into the birdhouse on the maple? I want to linger over every winged, petaled, leaved thing. I want to be permeated with the scent of growth. But living life means I miss so much.

"At some point in life, the world's beauty becomes enough," says Toni Morrison.

Not so. May is an assault. Too much, too much of everything.

The Vanishing Contractors

Spring meant that it was time to begin construction, starting with some comparison shopping. And that was when we learned about contractors.

Contractors, we learned, come in two varieties: those who can but won't and those who can't and won't.

Our future house was a case study in contractor limbo. For the builders with a decent reputation and a track record, it was too small. There was simply not enough profit in it. So we moved on to the local, one- or two-man operations.

These guys showed tremendous interest. They came, with their wives, children and dogs. They walked the property with us and marveled at the views. We all sat at the picnic table while I served drinks and cookies, and we chatted amiably. We learned all about them, their children, and their widely branching families going back generations, who they knew in our area and whom they were related to. We were dumbfounded by the intricacies of relationships in small towns.

It was all so warm and cozy. I wished to be adopted into one of these large families. There was an element of selfish interest here, since then we'd have had builders in our family, which at this juncture was preferable to the doctors and dentists we happen to have.

As the sun would begin to skirt the tops of the Adirondacks, they would be finally willing to take a peek at the architectural drawings. They made mysterious sounds that I took to mean approval, maybe admiration for the cleverness that was so obvious to us. They listened to our avid descriptions of the elements that would make this house green and organic, with a mitigated footprint that would scarcely blemish the hill. They nodded sagely when we explained how the passive solar heat would work seamlessly with the wood stove, how the air exchange system would save energy, and how the placement of windows would provide natural cooling.

By the time each contingent left, looking pleased and promising to be in touch within days, we were convinced that this guy or those two or that nice older man would be the one.

But none of those promising contractors ever called or returned our calls. After the first such experience, we wrote it off as an aberration. After the second, we began to question ourselves.

"Do you think it's us?"

"I have no idea," Ted admitted.

After the third, we were convinced it was us. But what were we doing wrong?

"Maybe we just come across as too aggressive," Ted ventured.

"You mean like driven, Type A, city people?

"Maybe the two of us are too much. With the next one, you do all the talking and I'll just smile encouragingly," I offered.

And that's what we did, almost, since I was less than perfect at being a wallflower. Still, the fourth one didn't call back.

It was truly bewildering. They were so enthusiastic. Why did they reject us? Or the house? Or both? Above all, why, oh why did they waste so many hours of their time and ours in what appeared to us as a charade? Did they have no work and therefore time to waste? If so, why were they not interested in the work we offered? If they were busily at work on other projects, why did they spend most of a day with us? No matter how we manipulated this puzzle, there was not a single logical answer.

Then, in the midst of utter befuddlement, we found Sam. Or rather, he found us.

Sam was tall, dark and handsome with a gentle voice and formal manner. He spoke in long, complex sentences, and he cited poetry. Sam had class. He understood our desire for a green house and wanted to see our dream come true. He had never built a whole house, but had lots of related experience and his references were impeccable. It seemed everyone loved Sam, and no wonder.

We quickly worked out a contract, at a higher price per square foot than anticipated. But Sam had various cost-saving ideas that would be instituted once construction was underway. Over handshakes and a lovely meal, which Sam consumed elegantly with fork and knife Continental style, he promised that work would start before the ground froze.

It was a long, warm autumn and the ground didn't freeze until just after the new year. And yet, Sam, now our special friend and confidante, the vital partner in our dream, had not yet stuck a shovel in the ground.

He was trying, he assured us, and I wanted to believe him wholeheartedly. It was those uncouth excavator guys who were being uncooperative. They promised to come and he went to meet them and then they didn't show. When they did show, they gave him estimates that were so outrageous they would throw the entire budget into the toilet.

"How," Ted asked, his voice unnaturally patient, "will you get all the other subcontractors... the plumbers, electricians, roofers, painters, and on and on, if it's so very difficult to get an excavator? Off season?"

Ah, but that was no problem. Because except for the excavators, Sam was well known in Vermont's building industry and subcontractors were eager to work with him.

"Let's then get an electrician and maybe he can get an excavator to trench for the electric lines," Ted suggested, speaking too slowly.

I felt bad, downright guilty when I saw Sam's expression. He was hurt. But he agreed to bring an electrician the following week. I waited till the end of the week to learn what I already knew. The electricians were all busy until spring. But why? Isn't winter their down season and spring their busy season? I wondered but didn't ask.

Unable to handle the pain I knew would follow for Sam, I allowed Ted to make an executive decision. We sent Sam a check to cover his months of work on our behalf, work that had robbed us of time and yielded nothing. It was the least we could do.

I was prepared to consider a radical departure from the plans without conceding the goal. I broached it tentatively one morning on the sunny cabin porch. Knowing that Ted disliked change, I was careful to establish an acceptable context, then dropped the doozie in the middle of this calm contextual pond.

"I was thinking..." I began slowly.

Ted's ears twitched in anticipation. This introduction, he knew, led to some curveball.

"No, I really think you'll like these thoughts," I ventured.

"I'm ready to move on from building a house." I didn't feel there was a need to review all the reasons. We both understood that our vast inexperience, exacerbated by Vermonters' peculiar attitude toward business, were reason enough.

"Are you suggesting we live here, in the cabin?" He appeared cheerful at the thought. Such a life would affirm his revulsion at our acquisitive culture. "We could, you know, install plumbing, and..."

"No!" Cabin living was a wonderful adventure for weekends and vacations, but this was 2007, not 1977, and we were past fifty, not twenty. "That's the same kind of thinking as when you wanted me to sew floor pillows instead of buying furniture. It's ridiculous!" I was losing my calm, which I needed to hold onto to introduce this new thinking.

"I meant that we should give up on this property, sell it, and buy something with a house on it that we can rent. Until we're ready to move."

There, it was out.

Ted didn't react as expected. He was looking away, silent.

"We could find another property we would love with a house already on it, I'm sure," I persisted, not at all sure.

Still, he was lost in thought, uncharacteristically silent.

"It would save us all the ..."

And then he interrupted with his own doozie.

"If we can't live here, then I don't want to move at all. Anywhere."

"What? What are you talking about? Why not?"

No answer.

"Anyway, this whole thing was my idea!"

He still sat there silent, infuriating.

"Why are *you* becoming so obstinate? So irrational? It's *my* dream!"

"This is how I feel. We live on this hill or we stay in New York. I am tired of moving."

"But we don't even really live here."

"I feel like we do. Like we've been here a long time."

He was right. I felt the same way. Our childhoods spent moving across continents, our families' uncertain existence, our whole long rootless history had brought us to this hill where we could be at home. Ted had not only co-opted my dream. He had, rightly, committed it to that one specific dot on earth.

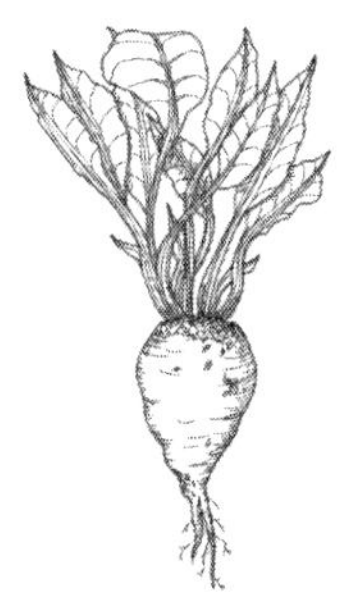

Deer

It's time to move Joe off my porch. I had sacrificed half an hour of a perfect spring morning to being neighborly. I am no longer listening to his right-wing tirade, when he turns the conversation to a topic near and dear to my heart.

"I planted a garden," he volunteers.

"Great! Where?"

"In the woods there," he says, gesturing north.

"How big is it?"

"80 by 80."

"80 by 80? You mean feet?"

"Yeah."

"But, that's huge! You must have cut a lot of trees! Why didn't you put the garden in the fields?" I ask.

"Better in the woods," comes the short answer.

This is truly baffling.

"Show me," I ask. I could satisfy my curiosity and move him off my porch.

He directs me to his ATV. I had never been on an all-terrain vehicle. Looking at the narrow space between Joe and the end of the seat, I have no desire to break that record.

"I can walk," I state nobly.

"Too far," he insists.

"No, really, I can walk forever."

"You'll get lost," he warns.

To this, I have no answer, since I had over time graduated from directionally challenged to directionally disabled.

Joe points behind him. I look at the woods, and at Joe, and at the short seat. Then I get on, trying not to touch him.

But as the ATV lurches forward, I am thrown against Joe. And thrown again and again as we swerve, bounce and tilt into narrow turns where one of my legs shoots up while the other bends against his side. Terrified, I clutch wads of Joe's clothing, and finally wrap my arms around his waist. My chin is hitting the back of his cap and my crotch is rubbing against his backside. Is it more terrifying or more mortifying? I wasn't sure then, but with the passage of time, the terror has faded while the appalling physical sensation remains vivid.

All nightmares come to an end. Climbing off, breathing deeply to contain the nausea, I stand at the edge of an impressive clearing.

"Wow, Joe, this is quite something! So much work!"

He nods, glancing down modestly.

"What did you plant? It looks like the same plant all over."

"Sugarbeets."

"Sugarbeets? What do you do with sugarbeets?"

"It's for the deer."

For the deer? Here is a stunning piece of information. Once again, I had misjudged, jumped to conclusions, wrongly indicted a decent person. Clearly, one could adore Rush Limbaugh while being kind and warm, a selfless person who devotes time and sweat to feeding deer. Contrite, I stare at Joe, and wouldn't be shocked to see a faint halo levitating above the John Deere cap.

Joe is pointing to a tree above us.

"That's where I sit."

"Where? Why?"

"See that plank? That's where I sit and wait."

"For the deer," he explains, since I am still looking at him dumbly. Then he surprises me, again, with this generous offer.

"I'll bring you some of the first one I get."

Field, Interrupted

Memorial Day. A workday for Otter Creek Builders. This is the first complete new house they are building since they established the company eighteen months before.

They are waiting in the warmth, pacing and smiling. The bulldozer has been parked at the bottom of the driveway for days. The sound of a truck rises from the road along with a cloud of dust. A door shuts. A minute later, we hear the bulldozer clanking up the driveway.

It moves into position and begins ripping off the earth's skin, marking out a brown square. As it digs deeper, the brown is streaked with the dead bluegray of clay. Within an hour, the bulldozer's cab is lined up with the ground where the six of us still stand. The men look cheerful. Ted and I look fearful.

Through a circuitous route spanning friends, colleagues, and friends of colleagues, we located a building company that seemed both competent and interested. Dan, Michael and Dave came to meet us in my office in Manhattan on a Sunday. Dan headed what for Vermont is a substantial company, whose construction subsidiary was headed by Michael. Dave was the master carpenter. They were in New York for the gallery show of a client. We took this to be a good omen. Even more encouraging was the fact that the three of them and their wives came together, as friends who socialized outside work.

"Crooks could never survive as both business partners and friends," Ted noted.

"Neither could three incompetent people who were being sued left and right," I agreed.

Here finally was a team with experience. They seemed genuinely interested in our house, at least as much as the friendly folk who had spent long hours at our picnic table. Most encouragingly, they looked at the plans within minutes of starting the meeting, understood them and the challenges involved, and even made useful suggestions to relay to the architect. They engendered complete confidence. Plus, whether due to our desperation or their charm, we liked them immediately.

Then, miracle of miracles, Michael called and emailed several times within just two days, and a week later sent a professional proposal, one that while needing lots of clarification and translation, seemed an eminently workable document. A meeting was set for the following weekend.

Sinking into layers of wet snow and muck, we limped up the hill with our bags. The ground had never properly frozen that winter due to the early and continuous snow cover, and by March had begun to turn into serious mud. The spring snowfall only deepened the mud. But the cabin warmed up within an hour instead of the several it took earlier in the winter, and stayed warm after the fire died out, which meant that Ted could sleep more than two hours at a time.

We were in high spirits when Michael arrived at seven Vermont time, which means a few minutes before seven. The plans were spread out over the beds and he began to explain the arcane terminology in the proposal.

The cabin was warm, the conversation relaxed, the sun streamed in. And the flies, which started out in the single digits during the night, were multiplying faster than our questions. From a few buzzing around the doors at daybreak, the population had exploded to proportions that would have stumped Malthus himself. The energetic ones covered every glass surface. The ones just reviving in the warmth buzzed lethargically on the floor where you could see them, and on the rugs where you couldn't, and on the apple-themed quilts and on our shoes and clothes hanging on the rustic pegs our artist daughter had fashioned from apple branches. They droned with a dull and horrible persistence, crawling toward every glass surface, squadrons of disgusting nuisance.

They were cluster flies, Michael explained. Later, when I looked them up, I learned that he was right, that they make their debut in autumn when they cluster on the sunny sides of homes in search of protected overwintering sites, and after cleverly surviving the winter become active on warm days, crawling out of wall voids and attics in a confused attempt to go back outside. But on that morning, I didn't care about the specificity of their species or their marvelous adaptations.

"Out!" I yelled. "I'm outta here!"

The air was saturated with melting snow. With windows and doors flung open and the fire dying, the flies would be dead by evening. Meanwhile, our discussion had to continue at the diner.

Munching on the diner's famous onion rings, we learned the meaning of fascia, R-values, electrical amps, and most importantly, the rough definition of budget allowances, a definition that would be repeatedly and severely amended over the next seven months. We also learned that the house, as depicted in the architectural drawings, is merely the skin stretched over the bones. And that before we could admire the miraculous raising of the house, there would be months of dull work involving such prosaic projects as developing a site plan, building a septic system, digging a new well, trenching electric lines, digging a foundation and pouring concrete. And that all these will not only be costly; but as Michael lucidly explained, were not part of the square footage cost calculated by the architect.

There was no argument about the need for electricity and water and a plumbing system. The foundation and concrete were less obvious needs to me, but I had to accept them at face value.

The proposal was refined but our changes, designed to increase the specificity of the job and the billings and provide a rudimentary guarantee in the form of a simple contract were ignored. We were still far from an acceptable contract in early April, when Michael and Donny came to examine the site.

"You want the house all the way up here?" Michael asked, incredulous.

We assured him that was the plan, and had been all along.

"What about the road?" he asked.

What about it? We didn't see what the problem was.

Michael was patient. The driveway, or road as it's called in Vermont, would be some quarter mile long. It will require frequent plowing, regular coverage with crushed rock, and keeping down of weeds, all of which would come with great expenditures of sweat and money.

Snow was a given, resurfacing and weeds were a new wrinkle. Still, no way was I going to let *weeds* force our house from its rightful place!

Michael looked at us quietly for a full minute. He asked Donny to drive the truck up and begin digging test holes.

After a few tries, he had his case sewed up. The hoe scraped its teeth on ledge almost immediately. Under a thin covering of soil, the hill was rock. Mostly slate, soft and easy to remove. This was no news; this area was after all known as "Slate Valley" and mined for a century for that reason. But underneath the slate, there was something harder, something more elemental. Granite, a rock tough enough to frustrate the forces of geologic time from leveling the hill into the valley below us. The same granite that glimmered from the top of Birdseye, the granite that survived the onslaught of the glaciers and gave the mountain its distinctive profile.

"They build houses right into mountains, carving them into the rock," I persisted. "Surely you can build a house on this flat area, even with rock underneath."

"Sure. But blasting through four feet of granite will cost," he assured us.

"Cost how much?" Ted asked.

There was no answer. Because, Michael noted, until they blast, they don't know what they'll find. So it could cost $25,000 or less. Or $125,000 or more.

"Depending," was the final verdict.

This was no small wrinkle. This was a major fold, a veritable rift in the fabric of our plans. This called for serious thinking.

The decision had to be put off for a week, two at most.

That week was devoted to coming to terms with this hard-to-swallow new fact: the spot on which we had for four years imagined our house was not where it would be. No driveway up the knoll, cutting through the graceful curve of a stone wall edged with lilacs and hydrangea, up to a shining house on the hill. The forest will not frame the western windows. Birdseye will not take center stage on the east.

We had to let go. The house would have to be below, closer to the road with a driveway half as long. Instead of forest, we'll see the Adirondack peaks. Birdseye would be visible, off center. All in all, not a terrible compromise. It wasn't until our first summer in the house, when our neighbor set up camp with a rusted trailer and a chemical toilet, nakedly visible from the original site, that we were thankful for whatever forces intervened on our behalf.

On the third Sunday in May, still with no contract, we cordoned off a two-acre area with hot pink tape. All the machinery and movement would be kept within this circle. In the center was the cabin, surrounded by the one hundred baby spruces I had planted the spring before. We potted up some and moved them to a kind neighbor who graciously volunteered to mother them for the season. The cabin would be moved later.

"Next time we come, we'll find total destruction here," I remarked.

"You can't expect them to build a house without destroying a blade of grass," was Ted's expected response.

A blade of grass. I had seen enough construction of suburban developments to fill me with dread. The serenity would be desecrated with clashing, cranking metal and growling machinery. The grass, already tall, and the buttercups just showing their shiny faces and much else would be crushed under the merciless tread of machinery. The earth would be compacted into heavy, airless, dead clay. The bird nests cradling eggs would be smashed. The rabbits and mice would be displaced. Only recently had the destruction wrought with cutting the trees been mended. And now, all the life that constituted the ecosystem under these two acres of grass would be ravaged. No matter how hard we tried to mitigate our footprint, it was going to be immense. I was desolate with guilt.

That evening, Ted raised the subject again, the one that we had examined, dissected and analyzed until it had become taboo: how to mesh the imposition of a new house on open land with our environmental principles. Is it ethical, we asked, to develop the land for our personal enjoyment?

I reasoned – rationalized? – that the land was for sale. Someone was bound to buy it. It's not protected land. The orchard and now the grassland were merely the latest imprint in a chronology of human interference over hundreds of years. It had been used to feed people for generations, for grazing sheep, then cows, and most recently, to grow apples. It hasn't been wild and unspoiled probably since Europeans began to settle the area, maybe before that. Even the grasses growing in wild profusion were hardly wild. All imports, the orchard grass, clovers and timothy. We were the land's best chance to enjoy some measure of protection. We would build a relatively small house, leaving all but an acre to revert to grassland or forest. In the process, we'd be providing needed habitat for ground-nesting birds. And, my clinching argument, we'd be preventing someone else from putting up something huge.

Ted did not totally buy into my argument. But he acknowledged that we needed a house. And he assuaged his guilt with his own rationalizing. A small green house would by some little understood alchemy help save the land that a conventional house would destroy.

In the end, the simple need for a house with indoor toilets put the arguments to rest.

Next morning I am at the construction site before the crew arrives. The future house's footprint is trenched four feet deep. I slide into the hole and walk the perimeter, observing the layers of topsoil, clay, shale. A firm foundation. Rising from the accumulation of eons. The peace is shattered by the arrival of a truck, followed by four more.

Time to let the grief and gift proceed.

Tree Rings

Watching the land being torn up was not a requirement. I needed time in the woods, alone, away from the infernal din.

I'm of average height, weight and age, but when I hike, I feel tall, svelte and young. Some friends are getting facelifts. Some are starting new careers. I go to the woods, and am restored to a younger self. The hikes I like best follow the ancient rounded mountains of the Taconics. Here, there are no soaring heights, shadowy canyons, or roaring rivers. It's a land of gentle rises and dips in dense hardwood forests punctuated by ponds and small streams. This means I can move swiftly mile after mile, taking huge steps and running jumps that let me feel the arc of the earth.

The earth's energy enters through my feet. Each toe finds its finely molded indentation. My knees bend to meet the earth's crust like a finely tuned feat of engineering. My arms swing long like an ape's. My body lengthens as it leaps over rocks and fallen trunks. I notice the flick of a whitetail a hundred tree trunks away, but don't stop. Miles turn into muscle, hours lengthen into sinews. I feel the running tide of my own blood.

The freedom of my legs gives freedom to my mind. It takes much of the four-mile trip to the usual turnaround point before its dartings form into a steady direction. It takes halfway back before all the noise in my head evaporates and my mind is empty, open to this close, forested world.

I'm always alone on this hike. Conversation of any sort or being forced to adjust my pace or stop to rest or eat when I'm not ready would turn the escape into a mere walk in the woods.

On this May evening though, I'd like to see another human being, preferably one with a flashlight, a cell phone and immense forest lore, the man of the woods himself. I started out too late, turned around too late, dawdled too long on the one ridge. Mostly, didn't realize how rapidly that warm disk in the sky retreats even this close to the spring equinox.

I'm at least two miles from the road. If I can make it to the lake, it'll be easy to follow the trail as it hugs the shore. After that, there'll be a narrow passage for a mile or so through thick stands of young white pines, but by then I may hear the road and follow the sound. Still. I'd never been here in the dark, or in any wild place without full camping gear. I'd rather not be here now.

Pushing on, my pace quickens to an athletic speed walk. Useless "if onlys" occupy my thoughts. If only I'd waited to plant the raspberries... if only I'd ignored that call... if only I'd left just an hour earlier, if I'd walked faster, eaten faster, turned around earlier. If only... I wouldn't be here after sunset, alone, wondering how long before the widely spaced blazes become invisible.

My fingers begin to tingle and my nose starts its inevitable drip, a sure sign that the temperature is sinking. I stop to drink the still hot tea, grateful that I packed it despite the promising day. But why not a flashlight? Part of my "take nothing extra," "keep it simple," "that's the beauty of hiking" principle. Snippets of repetitive conversations play themselves out in my brain.

"Sure you want to go alone?" Ted inquired, as he does every time. It's not that he wants to come with me, he's bored with the hike, but is willing to chaperone.

"Take the phone… take a flashlight…. what if it rains… what if you twist an ankle, what if… what if…"

Not that I deny that he's right and I'm foolish, but I choose not to be pragmatic. I refuse to believe that I'm anything but safe in these benevolent woods. So familiar that individual trees hold memories of themselves in spring flower or disrobing in autumn. So known that my legs mold themselves to the land's contours.

Still, my parents' sad voices echo in my swirling mind. Forests are dangerous. Forests are where our people were shot as they stood at the edge of the mass grave they had dug. Forests killed my father's young brothers as they marched through their frozen reaches. Forests surrounded Auschwitz, where my mother watched her mother and sister, clutching her baby, disappear into the line snaking toward annihilation. I love and fear the forest.

The shirt is sticking to my back. A wet cotton T-shirt will only exacerbate the cold. I sit on a ledge for another sip of tea. With fingers wrapped around the cup and the rock's warmth coursing down my legs and up my spine, a feeling of confidence returns.

"It's a perfectly gorgeous, calm evening," I reason. "What's the worst that could happen? Just go. Your eyes will adjust to the dark." Fixing the next blaze in my mind, I move into the night.

Assuming the trail is straight since the land appears flat, I feel my way across the uneven ground, my eyes anxiously searching for the next blaze. When I don't see it after what seems a reasonable distance, I retrace my steps to the ledge. I start out again bearing to the right this time where there seems to be an open line through the trees. Moving gingerly through the opening, I'm lost again. Looking up in desperation, I notice the faint white blaze on the tree in front of me.

Finding the next blaze proves more arduous. Following a hill, not big but steep, the trail seems to plummet. I know this cannot be, since trails are designed to take the path of least resistance. I scamper down and back up three times before finding the narrow opening.

My fingers are tightly clenched in perspiring palms. My back is stiff with cold or tension or both. My eyes feel distended from the effort of peering into darkness. Breathing rapidly, I give in to panic.

"At this rate, I'll wear myself out long before I get close enough to hear the road, or even reach the lake." Then, I order my frazzled mind, "Calm down. Stop panicking, stay calm."

I repeat the last phrase like a military order, playing it over and over until it forms itself into a silly little ditty I sing. For a little while I respond to this rhythmic mantra. My feet shuffle along slowly, toes pointed inward to keep from sliding on the slopes. When I get tangled in limbs and blackberry vines, I know I've lost the trail again. I yank at my clothes wildly, cursing the bushes.

Free at last, I push on. My entire being is now focused on getting from one blaze to the next. A mere hundred feet define success or failure, maybe even survival. As the night deepens, the tingling begins to reach beyond fingers and toes up legs and arms. I can feel that my ears are bright red. And the moon, the moon promised by the day's perfect sunshine ... it's either a new moon too tiny to notice in an old forest or else clouds had come up that will keep it shrouded for as long as it matters to me.

"If only I had a flashlight, or a single match... A cell phone!" But when I really consider these logical objects that should have been in my bag, I discard them one by one. The phone wouldn't work here. A flashlight wouldn't illuminate a large enough slice of these dense woods. And what would I do with matches? I'm incompetent at building a fire that lasts beyond minutes. If I did succeed this one time I'd probably start a conflagration.

Continuing to blindly put one foot in front of the other, I worry about Ted worrying about me. He's probably trying to figure out how to get to me. I can hear his heavy steps pacing the length of the cabin. These blend with the great volume of sound of each step on dry leaves. Together they join the cacophony in my brain. I sniffle and start running, tripping over a log and into a trunk.

I know I'm over the edge when I begin bargaining with fate.

"If I get out of here unharmed, I'll take every precaution in the future. I'll never leave with less than ten pounds in my pack. I'll buy a GPS. I'll leave a trail of glow-in-the-dark crumbs."

The bargaining takes on absurd proportions.

"I won't hike alone for the rest of the year…" Then, "not until next fall…" Until finally, I agree to never hike alone again, a promise I know even as I think it I have no intention of keeping.

Occupied with thinking up more outlandish bargaining chips, I step into water, and slush through it unaware until my boots are caught in deep muck. Quicksand! I scream, once, and again. Stay calm. That's what one's supposed to do in quicksand. Instead I continue to scream and thrash, away, back, forward, anywhere away from the life-sucking muck.

Hauling myself up to a boulder, I slowly collapse onto my haunches, my face between my knees, my eyes squeezed tight against my own foolishness. I know for a fact that there's no quicksand nearby. Just as surely, I know that I've lost the trail, which crosses no wetland.

I remove the slimy boots and socks, and wrap my feet in the small nylon pack. Uncorking the thermos, I sip at the last of the tea. There's nothing to do but wait for rescue. My head finds a hollow in the trunk behind me where it fits as into a favorite pillow. There's a stony calm. The forest and each living thing in it exists in and for itself. I sit alone in a heap of exhausted limbs, longing for my own kind.

Closing my eyes, I breathe deeply, and the aroma of millions of drying leaves, of the earth alive with crawling insects and burrowing mammals, of dew forming itself into droplets filters in.

A large dim nest sits in the crook of an upper branch. I hear the birds shifting in their sleep. A frog splashes into water, and I hear its webbed feet streaking through the shallows. I hear the papery rustle of leaves, each a unique note in the murmuring symphony of the living forest. I hear squirrels' tails wrapping around branches, moths struggling in spider webs, roots pushing relentlessly through the earth.

Beneath the craggy boulder on which I sit, I feel the miles of solid bedrock separating me from the boiling core of the earth, sustaining me now with retained warmth and solid presence. I feel the heady spinning of the earth and of my own astonishing presence on this grand planet.

Minutes or hours pass. When I open my eyes they fall on the smooth surface of the cut log in front of me. I can count the tree rings in the log. Then realize with a start that the clean slice can only mean one thing: I'm sitting right by the trail, now lit by serene moonlight that had come down unnoticed over the land. I can get up, walk out. I can, if I want to, flow over the land silently, snaking sinuously between the trees, making no disturbance.

But not yet. My body feels warm and ageless. My brain shivers with joy. I feel like putting down roots myself.

Septic Solutions

"What do you mean, no inspections? Doesn't the town come and look? To see if it's done right? That the house doesn't collapse or blow down or something?" a friend involved in many expansions and remodeling of restaurants around the world asked. We assured him, despite his disbelief, which had raised his voice to a shrill pitch, that the answer was definitely no.

No. Neither the town nor the state was interested in the integrity of the house. Neither cared whether it would stand up to the gale-force winds, whether it would sink during one especially muddy mud season, whether its electrical systems would short and catch fire, or if it had smoke alarms. We were free to poison ourselves and our unsuspecting guests with toxic water from the newly dug well or have the house burn down from a striking bolt of lightning. Nothing, nothing was required. Only a general building permit, based on nothing but our plan to build. It's a small town, an official explained, and like most small Vermont towns, without the resources to do house inspections. So an infinitely long rope was handed to us. With just one kink in it.

The septic system. In Vermont, the septic system can be the death knell of a proposed house. I'd heard of hundred-acre properties that were rendered undevelopable due to insufficient "perking," which precluded a septic system. On this, both the town and state were eager to weigh in, demanding multiple forms, even a formal visit.

Digging through the state government's website and reading through its publications, we learned that something called Act 250 was responsible for this surreal situation.

Created in 1970, this pioneering land-use law governs how major developments occur in the state. It has been successful in safeguarding the pristine environment, keeping out billboards and most big box stores, polluting industries and traffic-inducing residential development. All well and good. But exactly five weeks after we broke ground, the law was expanded to all construction, including a modest-sized single-family house surrounded by forty acres of open land.

This new requirement was complicated by the fact that no clear approval process had been devised by then. This minor hitch did not, however, delay the implementation of the law. The fact that no one – neither town nor state, nor builder, architect, site planner or excavator – understood the requirements or the various and sundry forms that had to be filed, with whom they had to be filed and by whom approved, had no bearing on the matter. And so we were privileged to become one of the first guinea pigs in the enhanced implementation of Act 250.

Finding a site for the septic field was the first challenge. It had to perk at a certain rate, meaning a set amount of water had to percolate through the soil and disappear within a specified time. Because so much of the soil in Vermont is rock ledge or clay that becomes waterlogged instead of allowing water to perk through, many wonderful house sites cannot have a house built on them.

Fortunately, we had made sure our property perked before we bought it. Unfortunately, the spot that was tested was hundreds of feet away from the new house site. The other spot was up an incline, requiring the effluents to be pumped up, creating an artificial hill and obscuring the woods to the north.

The site planner maintained these were absolutely the only spots with enough soil. I mentioned that while planting spruce seedlings I noticed pretty good soil closer. Not that I meant to tell him how to do his job. But still.

After more investigating, this closer spot, which needed no complicated pumping system since it was downhill from the house site and happily hidden from view, was deemed adequate.

Once, it was possible to bury a septic tank in the ground and be done with it. But now, only a mound system was permitted, consisting of a very large excavation that holds an elaborate piping system buried under many truckloads of fill and creating a mound several feet high. Simple, but the time and materials involved are impressive. And that was not all. Because one good site was no longer acceptable under the new laws. Now a replacement site was also necessary, just in case the site that was approved turned out to be wrong.

Once both sites were determined, it was time to begin the permitting process. The people responsible for granting the coveted permit were almost as lost as the site planner. The site planner reached the limits of his patience after completing three separate and very tedious forms, each with multiple illustrations. I proceeded to many polite conversations with state personnel, who patiently explained the process. The problem was, the process was explained differently by different people, and even by the same people at different times.

Meanwhile, with all relevant parties on board, there was no time to wait for approval. The system would be constructed according to best practices, while hope sprang eternal that these same practices would apply to the new permitting process.

But Michael couldn't find the spot. Maybe the site planner's map was unclear. Maybe one or the other was directionally challenged. The planner, I was told, had to return and stake the spot. But he was away, traveling, somewhere, with a vague return date.

In the meantime, construction was proceeding. I sent cheerful emails to the absent planner, hoping he would at some point check on his business. I was careful to keep hysterical notes out so as not to ruin his vacation.

"The house is framed!" I wrote. "But as you know, we can't dig the septic until your plans are approved. Any idea where that stands?"

"Great news. Michael called to say the septic tank is arriving this week," I enthused. "But he needs you to tell him where it should go." A tank was still needed uphill from the mound.

And finally, "I heard you're back! Please call me."

He didn't call, but finally emailed, promising to "jump" on the project.

One morning a backhoe lumbered up the driveway, turned a full circle, and trampling everything in its path, headed downhill toward the septic site. All day it lifted jawfulls of soil, dumping them on the perimeter of what – at some forty by twenty feet -- looked like yet another house site. As it headed back in the afternoon, it carved out a new path of destruction. Then it turned downhill again, but this time, its maw dug a trench from the house to the septic field. All day, watching the systematic rape of the field, I couldn't ask any questions; the operator was shielded behind thick glass and the surge of the screaming engine. I waved at him to cease and desist. He waved back at me cheerfully. I raised my arms, crossing and re-crossing them in what I thought was a universally understood motion. But the man continued to smile and wave.

When we returned the following weekend, the cavity was filled with a layer of crushed rock. Over these, an elaborate system of pipes wound its way in a beautiful geometric design.

"It's huge!" I enthused.

"Enough for a small hotel," Ted agreed.

"Or at least a full-service country inn."

"Why do two people in a three-bedroom house need this?" he asked.

"You know all I did was the paperwork."

"And this is what they demanded?"

"I don't know. The site planner submitted drawings. Guess they'd have told him if they were wrong." I was beginning to doubt my memory of the convoluted process.

"But no one knows what's right or wrong."

"But this is rather fascinating, don't you think?" I asked.

"It's rather expensive for no good reason, is what I think."

"I just hope this is how it's supposed to be done..."

The following week, after hand delivering yet another set of drawings and signing multiple pages, the coveted septic permits were granted by some mysterious higher authorities at both the state and town.

A date was set to test the system. The site planner came early, uncharacteristically merry. The contractor and the three carpenters working in the house asked to be notified when the town health officer arrived. I wondered what all the fuss was about, and started worrying. Could it not pass inspection? Surely, it was massive enough to meet all our needs. And if it failed for some reason, then what? Would construction be halted? Could the whole enterprise be doomed?

By the time the town health officer arrived, I had worked myself up to a fevered pitch. I wanted the test, whatever that entailed, to be over. Instead, everyone stood around admiring the beauty of the project, a beauty to which I was oblivious. A bunch of piping in dug earth. More destruction.

The water was turned on. The men sat on their heels at the edge of the dug area. Then, nothing happened. Not wanting to ask questions and thereby hasten the bad news, I waited silently, watching the faces for a clue. And still nothing. No rush of waters, not even the whisper of a trickle-to-come.

It happened silently and suddenly. Out of every tiny hole strung every few inches along the piping, a clear fountain of water rose, spouting into the blue air, cascading back in a tall arch. Maybe one hundred fountains, a symphony of cascades, a massive waterworks worthy of a Roman piazza.

I loved it. And I wanted it to stay as it was.

"It's too beautiful to cover up, don't you think?" I asked, almost expecting a miracle. But I got only embarrassed guffaws. When we returned the following week, the Roman fountain was performing its task under four feet of fresh earth. Beauty thwarted to serve our inalienable right to the civilizing influence of indoor plumbing. In the shadow of the rapidly rising house that subverted the fields to serve our dreams.

Visitors

Our friends and family mostly stayed away from our new venture, waiting patiently for indoor plumbing. But a stream of neighbors, some motivated by plain old friendliness, others by curiosity, visited the cabin.

Once, a long time ago, before e-mail or cellphones or even wall phones, people showed up for impromptu visits. Today, with exponentially growing means of communication, people don't come unless invited for a specific date and time. We all understand that an open invitation to come any time is not an invitation.

Except in Vermont, where an open invitation means showing up any time, without forewarning. As we learned when neighbors came and stayed. For hours. Not just a couple of hours. Multiple hours, whole chunks of a day.

In our first year in the cabin, we invited a lovely elderly couple to come by "any time." We meant to make it more specific, but before we had a chance to do so, they showed up on a Sunday afternoon, driving up in the truck and spending long minutes sitting in it, presumably giving us time to make ourselves decent, leaving us wondering about country protocol.

Eventually they got out and came to the door, laboriously climbing the three steep cabin steps. We welcomed them sincerely, since we sincerely liked these folks, and warmly invited them to sit. We each sat on one of four hard wooden chairs and chatted amiably, albeit slowly.

We offered drinks. Hot, cold, plain, alcoholic. Brought out the nuts. They refused all food and drink. They just wanted to sit and be companionable. And talk, at a very relaxed pace. A question was answered, eventually, but it took many minutes of silent contemplation before words were spoken. And the words, when spoken, came at a pace so considered that I found my attention span had been exhausted in the wait and I missed the answer when it finally came. Consequently, to fill the silences, I chattered away, with encouraging nods from our guests.

This felt good for a while, because unlike an animated conversation with our New York friends, no one interrupted me. Neither was anyone animated. In fact, with the late afternoon sun streaming in, I caught Ted nodding off a couple of times, an accusation he fervently disputed later, insisting it was only one very, very brief nap.

The non-conversation kept pace with the sun, becoming steadily quieter and more diffuse, until we were down to meaningful grunts and heavy nodding. The chair became an instrument of torture. I longed to lie on the bed or get up and move. But they didn't want to walk. They were evidently happy just sitting in those hard chairs, being quiet. I offered cookies, raisins, hard-boiled eggs, canned soup, anything available without refrigeration on a summer day. But they were content to just sit in silent fellowship. Taking a very deep breath, I slowed my breathing, trying to match their shallow ones. Perhaps I dozed off too, because I began to enjoy myself.

We have been learning to speak more slowly ourselves, to wait for things to happen in their due time, to criticize gently, if at all. And although I may never learn the patience that many native Vermonters have, I have learned to appreciate their pace, one that allows thoughts to shape themselves before being voiced. And allows others' thoughts to sink in before being answered.

Not all the people we met became good friends.

Within months of closing on the property and even before moving into the cabin, when the house was still a vague mirage in our future, we had succeeded in amassing a short but impressive list of local enemies.

First was the contractor, who was anxious to put his expensive machinery to good use. The cabin needed plumbing, he stated. No outhouse, not even one with a composting toilet was permitted. "Town health code," he stated, clinching his argument.

Except that a quick call to the town health officer yielded a different answer.

"Yup, you can, as long as the outhouse is the specified distance from the road and from water," the officer said.

"Really? You're sure?" I kept repeating, looking a gift horse too long in the mouth. But I didn't want us to start off by angering the authorities.

"You can cover the whole place with outhouses," was the short and final answer. It was an encouraging nod to famous New England individualism. Do what you want, it's your land.

This was indeed good news, which I promptly shared with the contractor.

But in a small town, it doesn't pay to make enemies. The following week, in the town offices to discuss another question, I was referred to a woman who turned out to be none other than the wife of the banished contractor. We both pretended that we had no prior knowledge of the other. She was icily polite and helpful, and to her credit, thoroughly professional.

Then there was the farmer whose cows and bulls had roamed our property. He had an agreement with the previous owner: in return for installing a well to water his animals, he'd have the right to use the fields to graze them for ten years, with seven to go when we bought the land.

Problem was, this arrangement was unknown to us until a fateful morning weeks after we had closed on the property. All we knew was we couldn't live in the middle of a pasture with cows and belligerent bulls.

We therefore politely asked the farmer to stop by on any weekend. When he did, we sat him down in the cabin and after an extraordinarily long warm-up session, proceeded to give him the bad news, leavened with some excellent news.

"You can, if you like, use the top or the bottom of the property for the animals, provided you install a fence," Ted explained.

Instead of looking pleased, the farmer looked out the window for a long while, and finally offered this: "I can do that for you (For us? I thought we were doing him a favor…), but it has to be across here," he said, waving a hand at the window.

"Across where?" we asked, the hand wave being unclear.

"Right across there," he responded.

"You mean right across from the cabin?" I asked.

"Yes."

"And to where?" Ted asked, giving me a meaningful look.

"Across," came the slow reply, his hand slicing an arc in the air.

After a few more attempts at clarification, we realized that what he had in mind was nothing less than dividing the fields in half along their length. This meant that we would lose the use of half our property, have no access to the woods, and would be staring at or walking along a fence at all times. We explained why this would not be acceptable, and offered the other sections again. Nothing doing. Cows need water, and that's where the water was. He left angry, the worthless agreement crumpled in his hand.

This whole affair might have bitten the dust of short-term memory, if that winter, the farmer, in a sharp career change, had not become the town's highway superintendent. Forced over the ensuing years to have regular dealings with each other, our relationship has evolved from civility to grudging warmth. Living here year-round and making efforts to fit in, we are slowly becoming simply neighbors.

Hunting provided yet another opportunity for alienating entire groups of people at once. Hunting is a sacred activity in Vermont, one that for two months every autumn supersedes the rights to own property and the pursuit of happiness. Some of our neighbors and their relatives and their close and distant friends are hunters, and they had become used to having access to our property. This was not just open land; with thousands of apple trees littering the ground with their precious cargo, a clarion call to the deer population for many miles around, this was prime hunting land. And now we owned it, and were not inclined to having men and an occasional woman dressed in camouflage and carrying weapons, roaming nearby. This seemed quite logical to us and to anyone else we complained to, who were by and large Flatlanders like us. But it was not well received by the hunting population in the area. Who owned the land on paper seemed, understandably, irrelevant. The fact that they had for many years used this hill as their hunting grounds gave them a sense of ownership for a few weeks each year.

It wasn't the deer, we could have explained. It wasn't an instinctive revulsion toward killing the deer, which if eaten seemed acceptable. And it certainly wasn't an in-your-face exercise of ownership of this coveted land. But we didn't think we needed to go into the reasons, which, to us, were so obvious and logical. So we didn't, simply declining permission, politely. Apparently, coming across arrogant instead.

The upshot? We failed at becoming instantly popular. In the neighborhood and in the town. Possibly in the entire state.

We had much to learn.

Most of our visitors are not of the biped kind. And mostly that is a good thing. They come, they wander through the grass or in the air, they leave, and sometimes don't return for months.

The turkeys, as many as a dozen, stroll through at a regal pace every morning, the babies visibly adding girth by the day. Sometimes they stop and fan out their tails in the classic Thanksgiving pose. Then they meander into the woods. Just when I begin to view them as my wild pets, they stop coming for months, until they reappear, this time crossing the road to a neighbor's field.

Animals have numerous entries through the ancient deer-proof fence erected to keep them out of the orchard. Bucks with impressive antlers stand on the hilltop for long minutes, assessing the opportunities. Eventually they move to the apple trees that rim the fields. On mornings after heavy rain, their hoof prints form undulating lines across the driveway. They often spend the night here. I can tell this from the depressions in the tall grass, where the warmth of their large bodies lingers.

There are too many deer, even in these parts, which, compared to other parts of the country, fall statistically somewhere in the middle of the deer overpopulation problem. But they aren't denuding the forests, and my vegetables ripen without a fence. In the end, as a local writer pointed out, the right number of deer is the number people are happy having around.

One winter a prehistoric looking creature materialized on our front lawn, its gray-white fur barely perceptible in the snow, except for its hideously pink snout and a fantastic tail of pink rings strung together slithering behind it. The opossum looked about blindly, turned in several directions, and finally moved slowly into the fields by the garage, where it had perpetrated a major excavation the summer before.

A particular porcupine seemed to take to our porches, making itself at home on each at different times. I watched this surreal creature with its thirty thousand quills from inside, knowing (even before learning that porcupines are nocturnal and this one was likely rabid) that the porches can't accommodate the porcupine and us at the same time.

Rabbits stand around, moving only when we move. One juvenile cottontail spent an entire weekend hugging the cabin corner. Was it frozen in place by terror or did it hope to become a pet?

The large gray squirrels that became my personal nemesis as they depleted the birdfeeder in our old house have not followed us. Instead, we have small, reddish specimens that have so far stayed out of the garage and barn, where we've heard they can cause amazing damage chewing through plastic wiring.

But it's the ubiquitous field mice that define this place. When the snow melts, the empty fields are peppered with their small dugouts. When the fields are cut in early August, the earth is a frenzy of activity as multiple hundreds of mice scurry for safe haven. As long as they stay away from my bare feet and out of my living spaces, I tolerate the mice. Not that I have a choice. But I continue to despise them. Cleaning the outhouse one early spring, I reached for what looked like a large ball of unwound toilet paper as a large mouse *flew* off the shelf and within inches of my face. I was startled into terror at the flight of this earthbound animal, more so than when I encountered a bear in Yosemite National Park. Then, I managed to stay calm and back off. This time, my bloodcurdling scream brought Ted running from the bottom of the hill.

Day breaks early on our hill in spring. Before 5 a.m., before the sun crests the top of slumbering Birdseye Mountain, I am awakened by a windswell carrying the songs of our resident summer guests.

Robins and red-winged blackbirds are the first migrants to return from their winter grounds in southern states. The male blackbirds, brash in their shiny black armor and bright red epaulets, arrive first to stake out territory, followed by the modestly colored females. This sets off frantic courtship displays, with males trying to prove they are the biggest, flashiest around, sometimes settling matters with high-speed chases. Then they settle into domestic bliss, until the younger males arrive. The older males defend their homestead while the females occupy themselves with nesting duties. The young males, chased away from nests and females, hang out in bachelor flocks and wait their turn for territory and brides the following spring.

After the blackbirds, the sparrows appear, bustling about without cease and with no apparent plan. The song sparrows, while drab in color, are the unchallenged virtuosos. Each sings a thousand variations a day on his basic twenty melodies. And each bird has his own repertoire, slightly different from others, each a creative artist. When not used to woo a mate, the songs, delivered with feathers puffed and wings raised, are used to defend his territory.

Hummingbirds, mourning doves, goldfinches, robins, bluebirds, clouds of swallows, wild turkeys, hawks make their home on the hill. They range from the tiny ruby-throated hummingbird averaging just three inches to the almost three-foot long red-tailed hawk.

But none is as important from an ecological point of view as the bobolinks. Members of the blackbird family, they are so named because of the bubbly song they sing in flight. They arrive to do what birds do in late spring – make more birds. The male, feathered in elegant black and cream with a puffy yellow head, sits on an isolated shrub or thistle, launches skyward, issues his song, and flutters his wings as he flies across the field. Apparently, this is a major turn-on for the ladies (and for me, too). After raising a flock, they spend the rest of the summer bobbing about and going through a molt that leaves both males and females a drab beige. As they fly south, they fatten up on harvested grainfields and fallow land, looking like tiny butterballs. Until they were protected by law, they were killed and eaten on their way to their winter habitats in South America.

A wildlife biologist with the Vermont Institute of Natural Science, studying bobolinks in their wintering grounds, described how they erupt from the rice fields in Bolivia by the tens of thousands, their noise making the annual uproar of spring peepers seem like a whisper.

They fly some six thousand miles -- an astounding feat for a bird that weighs an ounce. One female, known by researchers to be at least nine years old, presumably logged a hundred and ten thousand miles, the equivalent of circling the earth four and a half times.

But despite their aerial prowess and charming song, all's not well with bobolinks. Their numbers have been declining, plummeting almost fifty percent in the last four decades, according to the North American Breeding Bird Survey. These are grassland birds, and cornfields and hay fields have largely replaced the prairies and uncultivated fields that are their natural habitat. When fields are cut before the babies fledge, an entire season of breeding is shredded in the blades.

Things are even worse a continent away. Contrary to the way we welcome them back to Vermont, bobolinks are viewed as pests in the rice fields of South America. Here, congregating in enormous flocks, it's easy to exterminate thousands at a time. Pesticides used on rice, even if not intended specifically for the birds, are extremely toxic to them. Widespread development in their wintering grounds is yet another scourge that threatens these beautiful birds.

These conditions affect not only bobolinks. All the migrating birds that populate North America for part of the year are being decimated by a perfect storm of negative conditions: loss of habitat here compounded by loss of habitat in their wintering grounds, worsened by pesticides used on crops and by outright extermination by agricultural interests.

Half the answer lies in our eating habits. Produce imported from Latin America is three to four times more likely to violate Environmental Protection Agency standards for pesticide residues than the same foods grown in the United States. Simply put: imported fresh produce in winter means fewer bobolinks in spring. I can resist those unnaturally enormous raspberries in winter, but who knows where the rice and quinoa on my pantry shelf come from?

Casting a Shadow

Building a house is a lot like raising a child.

There are all the months of gestation, when the only sign of the human to come is an expanding abdomen and faint kicking. Once born, progress is rapid. Within the first three months the infant is transformed from an alien looking, vegetative being into a tiny full-fledged person who responds with smiles and musical cooing. Just weeks later, the infant is turning over, holding the bottle, flirting. Then after the first year, the heady rush slows to an observable process.

A full month had passed since the cabin had been moved up the hill to make room for the rapidly evolving house. And since our last attempt to hammer out a contract with Michael, even a sketchy one. Our changes on each new version were met with the same solution: let's do T&M (time and materials). Let's not, we insisted. We need a number. Even if it's a moving target that ratchets up daily. T&M would deprive us of even the illusion. It would turn us into control freaks who would obsess about the length of the lunch breaks and the trips to the hardware store.

We made several more half-hearted attempts to work out something Michael would accept, but it was mid spring, the subcontractors were lined up and ready, figuratively pacing the perimeter. It was time to build, contract or not. A friend described how his addition, which was roughly the size of our house, was agreed on over a mere handshake. (He later sued the contractor for unfinished and shoddy work.) We took a leap of faith that could have ended in crushing disaster. But over the next seven months, as the house rose, so did our confidence in Michael and his crew. Visitors who knew more than we did confirmed that the house was being built with enormous care and attention to detail. A clear case of beginner's luck.

Once again, we divided up the research and decision-making, thus mostly avoiding marital discord. The labor was equitably divided. The one with the least talent, experience and interest in a particular area got to nominate the other to that project. Thus, since I knew or cared even less than Ted did about the heating, electrical and other systems, these became his to try to understand. All finishes -- from paint colors and floor tiles to staircase design and window framing -- became mine.

The daily communication with Michael also fell to me. After the first few encounters, the two pronounced male egos began to raise hackles and other unpleasant things and were clearly not about to form a warm bond. Being a woman, I found it easy to dispense regular ego massages, keeping all the wheels properly lubricated.

Months of excavating and earth moving, of trenching and compacting, of pouring foundations, embedding footings, and raising of frost walls left me impatient. All these months, all these checks, and still nothing, or at least nothing that led me to believe a house would soon, within the promised time frame, rise on the spot.

One late-summer weekend we walked inside the perimeter of the four-foot–deep hole, only our heads above ground. The layers of earth were now all gray cement, not conducive to aesthetic visions. The following Friday evening we hopped around on the girders and across the foundation walls that divided the space into rooms that until now had existed only on paper. Long after the sun had set, we climbed in and out of the "house," and walked from room to room, admiring the view from each, jumping across the low walls, a couple of awkward Gullivers.

I stood a long time in the kitchen, peering at the Adirondacks, seeing myself at the future sink in that spot. The prospect of a built house seemed suddenly more than possible.

By the following week, piles of wood were heaped on the ground beside the foundation, a shocking amount of fresh lumber, maybe half an acre of forest chopped, peeled, cut, sliced and delivered to build this one modest-sized house. The siding would be cement board, the floors ceramic tile, the construction stick and not post-and-beam, saving who knows how many trees. And still, the amount of wood was shocking.

Then magically, as we rushed up the driveway the following Friday evening, full-sized walls rose to greet us. They were mere bones, an intricate skeleton built of two-by-six lumber, but there was no doubt; they formed the recognizable frame of a house, an admirable, larger than envisioned house. And just days after that, the floor girders and joists were in place, and the framing rose to the headers. We could no longer climb across the walls; we had to come and go through the door openings, and gaze through gaping window holes. We stayed long enough to see the moon rise and float to a focal point right above the center of the house.

In the morning, I watched a wavering stream of Monarch butterflies through the open roof. Then another, shorter stream, followed by a longer one. A couple of feet above the fields, just missing the tallest grassheads, were many lilting butterfly trails, all flying toward points south of Birdseye. Singles, pairs, a half dozen orange and black wings almost stroking the grass, rising on unseen air currents, turning the gray day shimmery. The migration continued all day, sometimes faltering to a few stragglers but then picking up numbers until the air was filled with silent winged movement. I was afraid to walk, afraid to hit these frail creatures, afraid they would hit me and shatter.

Every late summer since then I wait for the predicted Monarch migration. Their two thousand five hundred mile journey to Mexico's Sierra Madre starts somewhere north of us. They still have almost all those thousands of miles to go.

I rise early and watch intently for this otherworldly event. But each year, the numbers dwindle. Illegal logging in the Sierra Madre has slashed their numbers. Dry, Monarchs survive below freezing temperatures, but wet, they freeze to death in the damper, colder winters already produced by climate change. Finally, they depend on milkweed in their larval stage. Milkweed grows in fields, and as the available uncut fields in their summer habitat shrink, so do the Monarchs.

Up here, we need no scientific studies; the evidence is in the sad little groups of Monarchs that meander over our fields in September, a more terrible reminder of their demise than a total absence would be. I pray for these remnants. I pray for enough goldenrod and yarrow and asters to provide sustenance. I pray for no wild wind to tear off their wings. I look at the small spruces we planted as a windbreak. We'll encase each in a snug cocoon of burlap before winter arrives. But who'll protect the butterflies?

Waiting for the remembered profusion but ready to settle for a remnant, I try to recall the heartbreaking lines in "I Shall Never See Another Butterfly," penned by a young inmate in Terezin, a concentration camp in what is now the Czech Republic, where tens of thousands of children were held for months or years before being transported to death camps. I can only remember the last stanza. "That butterfly was the last one/Butterflies don't live here/in the ghetto."

Of course not. They barely live in our free world, free to destroy butterflies.

Once the girders were up, the work proceeded at a brisk pace. By the following weekend, the headers and beams were in place, followed by the roof trusses.

It was a thing of beauty, this skeleton. Built of varying widths and lengths of wood, lovely and rugged, delicate and sturdy, a genius of design. Like a suspension bridge or a series of moving gears, it was a show-and-tell of complex engineering. And as I would admire a newborn baby, so common and yet miraculous, I admired this cunning and exquisite creation, trusting that for all its seeming fragility, it will withstand the weight of sheetrock and of weather and of decades.

Two weeks later the roof was covered up. I wasn't sure I liked this new solidity. It shut out the sky. The space seemed confining. The large open playpen had been turned into a large cage of hundreds of bars. I wanted to see the moon drift across from the east to the west wall. Instead, the moon cast a huge shadow of the house across the barren earth.

The confinement though was a quantum leap closer to a cozy retreat safe from the elements. I could now walk from room to room and see our life in the house. Bread rising in the kitchen. Visiting children rising in the guestrooms. Future grandchildren peering laughing around doors. I could clamber up the ladder to the second floor and feel myself gratefully climb into bed. Coming down, I had visions of drifting through furnished rooms, straightening chairs and pillows, sipping tea. Instead of the mountain of weed-sprouting earth created by the bulldozer, I would be gazing at tomatoes and pumpkins glistening with dew, and birds cavorting in a birdbath.

There were still months of demanding work, heavy equipment and noise ahead. Trucks rumbled up the driveway, delivering more lumber, boxes and boxes of roof shingles, miles of wires and pipes, palettes of wallboard. How many nails had already been hammered into this house by how many multiple thousands of hammer strokes? How many hundreds of cuts had been made in lumber used in the girders and joists, the framing and beams? The activity was surging with the lengthening days.

Early in the spring, a couple of returning tree swallows had set up their domicile in a birdhouse mounted on the cabin. Four white eggs were laid. Perched for long periods on the birdhouse roof, facing thoughtfully in the same direction, the future parents stood watch.

Then the men and machines moved in. Ignoring the screeching, rumbling, tearing mayhem, the swallows remained on their roof, stolid, determined. At times, one would fly off and the other would move into the house to wait. They met the clamor with outraged cries and low forays, swooping close to the men and machines before landing back on their perch.

One of the young carpenters built a three-legged stand and positioned the birdhouse on top of it. There followed an afternoon of wild protestations, with mama and papa circling their house in its new location, emitting a cascading series of complaining calls. By evening, having vented their opposition, they moved into their old home in its new location. It was close enough, after all, and the eggs had not been touched.

The birds carried on, and so did we. We didn't know when the babies were born, but when the house seemed empty one day, I peered in and saw them. Three impossibly small and naked beings huddling in the far corner, pushing deeper away from my inquisitive gaze.

The family remained there through June and July. We watched the babies emerge one by one, and amid the roar of construction, leave on their maiden flight. One windy day, when we could see the bobolinks were holding on for their lives on the wildly swaying grass stalks, someone noticed that there had been no activity for days. The swallows had left, perhaps for saner fields, until their journey south.

Wind

The wind. It took years to comprehend its power. Even after we had been living in the completed house for a full span of seasons we continued to be shocked by its destructive force.

"Last night? Yup, the wind did blow," agreed our neighbor.

This left us speechless. Surely there was more to be said about the wind. After all, it had not just blown. It had whipped and howled, stormed and screamed. It had torn shingles off the roof and blown them to the bottom of the hill, plastering them against the fence. It had turned solid glass into liquid. We had stood watching the windows waving like quiet lake water, disbelieving our eyes.

"Am I imagining it?" I asked timidly.

"The glass IS waving, right?"

I moved toward the window, intending to put my hand on it, to verify with touch what my eyes saw.

"Come back!" Ted warned. "It could shatter on you."

Surely, this "wind event," as the insurance company called it, merited more than such gross understatement.

"But did you ever see such wind?" I persisted, waiting for something just a bit more dramatic, something that would validate the near terror that had stalked us.

Many seconds passed.

"Yup," he admitted, then stopped. After another minute had passed, he resumed. "I told you. Before. Before you bought the place. The wind does blow up here." And he picked up his cup of coffee again, signaling that he had completed his take on the wind to his own satisfaction.

He was sitting at the dining room table, a handsome old man with florid cheeks and a runny nose that he wiped with a red bandana. He had been sitting for nearly two hours, the time slowing to a pace that matched his speech. With my mind left whirling at the speed of the night's wind. Forced to sit. To contemplate at his measured pace. A much needed exercise in patience.

God, at the creation, is the wind moving over the waters. Wind is life-giving air, multiplied. Air is a sacred element for many cultures. It animates us. The soul itself is associated with air, leaving our bodies in a quick exhalation. In Hebrew, *neshama* means both soul and breath; likewise *anima* in Latin.

On a more prosaic level, the wind keeps our hill virtually free of the dreaded black flies and tormenting deer flies, even from mosquitoes, which some summer evenings are so plentiful they form a transparent gray cloud in the middle distance, prevented from reaching us. It spreads the seeds of the grasses and trees, maintaining the fields in their green glory and the forest expanding wherever we allow it. It keeps our house naturally air-conditioned during all but the most harrowing heat waves.

And yet, it can be a lunatic force, a fanatic, rampaging power.

The outhouse was the first to suffer its fury. Twice it blew over, the first time when our daughter spent a weekend in the cabin with friends. For some reason, they found the sight exceptionally humorous. I know this because I got a phone call from Daniela. Between her cascading giggles and the background hoots of the two other twenty-somethings, it was impossible to determine whether the structure was still lying on its back, its moon cutout staring at the open sky, or whether they had succeeded in righting it.

The second time, Ted and I found it on its back. I cannot explain what was so sidesplittingly funny in this sight. Whatever it was, it swept over us, until we too had to sit, then lie down on the frosted grass to catch our breaths.

Lacking upper-body strength, I was of no help pushing the outhouse back into an upright position. While Ted's side rose several inches above the ground, mine stayed securely stamped on the grass. Ted gave very specific instructions on where to put my hands and how to heave using my bent legs, which compared to my arms are powerful. My fingers, shod in heavy work gloves, remained too short to wrap around the corner, but he assured me that with proper control over the rest of my muscles, I could handle my side.

I couldn't. Pronounced useless, I suggested that what he needed were some strong young men. Sure, he noted, and sent me away dismissively to find them while he tied ropes around the prone structure.

"Sure," I answered flippantly, and turning my back on him wandered away, annoyed with my limitations. Despite all the exercise and healthy living, I am indeed useless when it comes to anything requiring muscle strength. The outhouse would need professional intervention, because finding a few young men was about as likely as finding a few banana trees among the apples. We hardly knew anyone. The college semester had not yet started, so even the rare car filled with young men was absent. And what was I supposed to do, anyway? Walk up to a burly student and ask him to find others like himself and then drive them to the outhouse?

But we do have a few neighbors. And one of them rents an apartment above the garage to college students. And not one, but two cars were parked by the apartment. And standing in the doorway, beer cans in hand, stood three young men, each a monument to youthful health and strength. Despite the fact that they had just finished helping their friend move in, they looked ready for a new physical challenge. I walked them up our hill like a mother duck with her overgrown ducklings following. Triumphant, I waved to Ted, who stood by the prone outhouse, stunned.

"I brought you some strong young men. Three of them," I said, smiling at Ted, at the young men, at the sky, at the world.

On another occasion, no young men, no matter how buff, could move the cabin back when it had been blown off the cement blocks during a Nor'easter. Professionals with huge equipment came, carving up the grass, and poured a cement foundation. Then they repositioned the cabin on its new altar. The following winter, the 2,600-pound cabin was again moved some six feet west, this time tearing the newly installed metal cables out of the foundation along with the lightning wires buried in the earth, flinging cables and wires away like so much detritus.

Asleep in the house, windows secured against the shrieking air, we heard none of the destruction as it was being perpetrated. Nor the snapping of the first of the newly planted apple trees that we had coddled for three years.

At its most violent, the wind blows from infinity, and there's no butte or hillock, no tree line close enough or tall enough to hold it back, nothing until it smashes against our house. We hear those enormous volumes of air that snarl in whirling tongues, that lash the million blades of grass into a flat wetness, that reel leaves up from the road to clump them in a corner, that laugh shrilly at the young evergreens we planted as a windscreen, that shudder the roots of the burdock.

Miraculously, always, within hours or at most a night, the wind drops its deafening pitch to a low, dark moan. The sun appears among rafts of clouds. The mountains gleam in their many splendored crags. We go outside to survey the damage. I walk to the garden and the orchard, Ted heads for the cabin to make sure the new monstrously heavy cables and the thick tree trunks that we've leaned against the cabin for added support are still doing their job. From there, he can also assess the house roof.

The world is washed in white light. The grass and flowers, after playing dead for the wind, are exhaling their perfumed breath. Walking back to the house, I notice that all the windows are newly scrubbed.

Not even watermarks. No flies, no mosquitoes, and clean windows. The wind drives a hard bargain. But I too feel like a winner.

Holding Pattern

The windows were installed just before Labor Day. The house was now sealed. When the siding was nailed in place and the roof shingles were laid, we had a real house. We could, if we chose to breathe dust and wood shavings, lay a sleeping bag on the cement and live in it.

Then the plumbers and electricians came with pipes and miles of wires that they wove throughout the skeleton. The shiny pipes with their perfect turns and arching reach toward future sinks and showers, the electric wires shimmying smoothly, erupting in short petals at future lighting fixtures, the air exchanger pipes that crisscrossed the walls and that would maintain the air quality in this super tight house, all these formed a varied canvas. But within days the insulators blew the canvas full of puffy stuff that hardened into a material looking nothing like I imagined the natural cellulose would look. This was covered with another layer of foam. Finally the sheetrockers arrived, and the now filled canvas began to rapidly disappear behind smooth gray walls.

This meant the end of heavy construction. We'd have relative peace. The soil around the house, compacted under tons of metal for months, would possibly begin to breathe again.

Until the moving truck. But that was still months away.

Because now came the part we'd been warned about, the "finishing." This seemed like a minor afterthought compared to the task of erecting a house, nothing but a swift interval before completion. In fact, it was a time consuming, highly detailed process that took twice as long as putting up the structure. And, whereas the basic building was completed without involvement on our part, the finishing called for long meetings with the electrician, the painter, the tile installer, the plumber. And daily demands for hundreds of decisions, decisions that had to be made by end of day, by next day or, at best, by next week.

I know exactly how many decisions we made because I kept a running list in a huge black binder, and when it was bursting, I went on to a white binder. By the time the house was ready for the final inspection, this list ran to an unbelievable, incomprehensible, unfathomable seven hundred and forty three entries, including summaries of seventy-three phone and in-person conversations. A dedicated email folder contained two hundred thirteen separate email messages. The binders were bursting with photos, plans, drawings, and notes filed under eleven separate headings from construction and windows (the least number of pages) to kitchen and miscellaneous, the two most bulky.

All this used up an unknown number of hours. What I know is that it resulted in three hundred sixty four hours of lost sleep, calculated at the rate of two a night, not including the months of design that preceded construction. The madness reached a crescendo during a single grueling "vacation" week dedicated exclusively to shopping for the house, during which I lost eight pounds in as many days.

Every minor or seemingly inconsequential choice gained importance as its due date closed in, until every decision loomed as a final and monumental verdict. How crucial is the style of the window framings? And the width of windowsills? How about the type of pine used? Can we get away with knots or must we have smooth pine? Given that the entire southern wall of the living room is glass, this decision rated high. But what about the hardware that cranks the windows open and shut? Surely these can't matter much. Ah, but they come in six styles and dozens of finishes. Poring through the catalog during the hour-long train ride to the office and during another hour on the way home, their import grew to absurd proportions. Surely, a company wouldn't offer all these choices if the importance of the hardware were not evident to everyone but me. So I pored and pored. The least expensive ones had an unwanted curve in them. Would this curve be an issue in a house built around right angles? Plus, it came in only three finishes, none of which was the cool metal I now knew the house should have.

I had entered the twilight zone of home design. It was mortifying to spend so many precious waking hours, and hours when I should have been sleeping but couldn't, on such petty matters. Surely, with what we estimated as the last ten good middle-aged years left, frittering chunks of them on window hardware was not a good use of time. But in this new zone, nothing was petty. Everything came with an astounding number of choices, everything had to "work" with everything else, and every potential mistake had repercussions on everything else. A second-best finish on the window cranks could do more than mar perfection; it could bring down the entire painfully wrought enterprise.

Our foray into the never-never land of bathroom fixtures was typical of the dilemmas we faced.

A late morning and an entire afternoon. Five hours, half a day. That's the time we agreed to set aside to choose fixtures for two and a half baths. That's three toilets, three sinks, two showerheads and a bathtub, plus faucets. It seemed a generous enough allowance, given that we had only six and a half days to pick paint colors, tiles, floors, lighting fixtures, closet doors, front door, kitchen countertops, all the appliances, lighting placement, porch windows, and dozens of other components we didn't yet realize went into a house, from light-switch covers to drawer pulls.

Arriving at the bath showroom, I knew we were once again unprepared, as evidenced by our aimless wandering with no discernible focus.

"Look at all these faucets. I had no idea there were so many. Who designs so many? They all look very similar," I marveled.

"Are you even looking?"

"I am looking at the prices," Ted responded.

"But why would this one cost $300 more than that one? They look the same, right?" I wondered aloud, not expecting an answer.

He mumbled something about the type of metal and country of origin, but it was obvious he had no satisfying explanation.

A young salesman came to us smiling. He had heard our exchange and explained that the difference lay in the design. One was simply better designed and therefore cost more.

I could see that, barely. One was a bit sleeker, and was available in more finishes. But it didn't warrant a three hundred percent markup. I said so. This didn't seem to please the salesman, who proceeded to point out the, to me, negligible improvement in the obscenely priced faucet. I nodded, and walked on among the faucets. He remained supremely polite.

"Let's start with the style of house," he offered.

This question was more complicated than it should have been.

"Well, it's kind of contemporary, but not really modern," I offered.

"It's not a farmhouse or a barn-type house or any kind of typical Vermont house," Ted added.

"It's a little like a prairie house, with a nod to Frank Lloyd Wright," I explained, nodding my head encouragingly. To myself or the salesman?

The young man also nodded, now looking as confused as we felt.

"I see. So what kinds of bathrooms did you have in mind?" he inquired pleasantly.

Again, we were at a loss. A bathroom with a sink, toilet and shower, I wanted to say, but knew this was not the right answer.

"Maybe we should start with the budget allocated to bathroom fixtures and we can go from there," Ted, ever pragmatic, suggested.

"Let's first walk around and show him what we like and he can tell us if it fits the budget," I suggested.

This turned out to very unpragmatic.

We started the process. Ted had no strong feelings for any particular toilet or showerhead. He sneaked outside and sat in the sunshine talking on the phone. I, on the other hand, became slowly entranced as my level of sophistication ratcheted up, admiring a particular curve on this faucet or the sweep of a soaking tub.

Minutes before the store closed I had chosen just about everything we needed, "just for size," as the salesman counseled, so he could begin to understand our taste and we could get a feel for the prices.

The proposal arrived the following week. It was nine pages long. The last page contained the totals, list and discounted price. Both were well into the five digits, with the lower more than fifty percent over budget. But I had all the catalogs, so all I had to do, the salesman counseled, was see what else I liked that was lower priced. But the prices were not listed. Not a problem, he explained. Just go with what I like. We'd work it out.

There was little I didn't like in these artsy catalogues, and the more time I spent admiring, the more my taste continued to be refined. Three times I sent a revised list. Each time, the proposal came back higher. Could it be that everything in the catalog came in two categories: very high and even higher?

Another trip to Vermont and the better part of another day spent at the showroom. This time, the plumber came along as facilitator. He asked pertinent questions and pointed out the less expensive copies for many of the original choices. Ted hung around this time, saying little but looking increasingly dazed.

"What's wrong with that faucet?" he'd ask, noting my unhappiness.

"Nothing is *wrong* with it, it just may not be the best choice," I would say, trying to stay patient. "There just may be another that would look better."

"It looks fine."

"Can't you see it doesn't coordinate with the showerhead?"

"No. They're the same metal."

"But one is matte!"

"So? They'll get along."

Despite his stubborn refusal to even try to develop the rudiments of my now discerning eye, eventually we had most everything picked out. Then came the color choices, and with that a new learning curve.

"Why is "Thunder Gray" twice as much as "Mexican Sandstone?" I asked.

"It's a new color," I was told.

I understood then. Sink and toilet colors are like drugs. The company developing them must amortize its investment up front, and the price will drop only after the color becomes generic and common in every low-budget condo development. For now, "Thunder Gray" commanded a steep premium. I could pay it or settle for "Vapor Blue," or even the lowest priced but to my now discriminating eye, "Barely Black" which was in truth barely gray.

Toilets are more complicated than sinks, involving more than just color and shape. They come in regular and comfort height. Does regular mean it's uncomfortable, I asked, and if so have I been uncomfortable my whole life? Could that discomfort-provoking toilet, used first thing in the morning and before retiring for the night, be the culprit that often sets the tone for whole strings of bad days? And if so, how could I not have known that there are life-altering alternatives to generically terrible toilets?

The answer was provided matter of factly. Not only were comfort-height toilets higher and therefore more comfortable (why wasn't clear to me and I didn't have the courage to ask), but they also came with an added feature.

"Look at this one, and now look at that one," instructed the plumber. I did. I saw no difference, except one was higher.

"Look at the outside of the bowls," he commanded. "Do you see the difference now?"

It took several more lengthy comparative observations, and then, I got it! The comfort-height bowl came with a smooth finish below the seat. All the undulating curves and bumps that apparently mar ordinary toilets had been removed from this improved model.

"I see it now, but what's the advantage?" I asked.

"This design is much cleaner, plus, it's easier to clean," the plumber clarified, bending to demonstrate by running his hands up and down the smooth sides, incredulous at my lack of appreciation.

The proverbial straw that broke Ted's dwindling patience was the toilet seat.

"Do you want regular or slow-close seats?" we were asked, just when I thought we were really, truly, finally done.

"What? What's the difference? We don't care," I said.

But there is a difference, and this was demonstrated with great fanfare. Unlike an ordinary seat that slams down with an uncouth sound when dropped, the slow-close seat requires only a gentle nudge from the user, who can leave safe in the knowledge that the seat and the lid – if so chosen -- will slowly lower themselves on their own, settling demurely with barely a sound into their predetermined positions.

Ted sighed very audibly. We looked at him.

"This is why our world is coming apart," he said, his voice tired, lacking the anger that should have accompanied such a significant statement. "I'll wait for you outside. You decide on the toilet seats."

I made a quick decision. The slow-close seats.

As if I had a choice.

Mustard

On the mustard plants that were turning our fields a lurid yellow there was only one way to decide.

It must be noted that this mustard is not an ugly plant, nothing like the monstrous burdock whose taproot reaches into the earth's bowels, or the outsized, thorny Canada thistle, or the nettle that hides its sting behind coy baby-green foliage. From a distance, its ranks are not very different from any golden field of cultivated flowers. If I remove my glasses, I can imagine that I'm seeing a bright field of black-eyed Susan.

Except these are not black-eyed Susan, nor even the wildly proliferating goldenrod. This is garlic mustard, a weed, an exotic, an invasive. It's the first in an army of foreign colonizers threatening the grasses and flowers that have covered our Vermont hill for a hundred years or more. And it's not a well-behaved plant, willing to share with others. It grows at an astounding rate, mutating within three weeks from a charming rosette into a tall, many-stemmed adult sporting a yellow inflorescence and multiple large seedpods. It hogs every inch of open soil, preventing anything else from growing, "a severe threat to natural areas because of its ability to quickly dominate the ground layer to the exclusion of native plants," according to a fact sheet published by the Vermont Department of Environmental Conservation, Fish and

Wildlife. It may even threaten some butterfly species, and it appears to degrade habitat suitability for native birds, mammals and amphibians.

If you sense some irrational hatred here, you're not wrong. Except it's not irrational. Those gloating golden heads earn the strings of hideous curses they wring out of my very heart. No emotion toward any living thing approaches the intensity of the evil I feel toward the mustard.

I didn't always hate weeds. A long time ago, when we moved into our first house, I felt quite kindly toward whatever grew on our suburban lot. The first spring, when the lawn came up rather sparse, I was not at all averse to the cheerful dandelions that filled in the bare spots. Why, I wondered, did people go to such lengths to eradicate such a bright little flower? Why should a lawn be a uniform green when it could be starred with gay dandelions? It wasn't up to me to assign relative worth to any one plant. Dandelions and fescue had the same right to live and thrive. Surely, mine was a more sophisticated approach to gardening, a harbinger of the demise of the manicured suburban lawn and the rise of the suburban meadow, and I fancied myself a trendsetter in this eco-friendly ethos. I even tried dandelion tea (green tea is better), and planned to make huge dandelion salads.

None of this happened, because well before the official start of summer, I despised dandelions. The compact little plants had grown into leggy teens, weaving on weak stems far above the grass, their tops large globes of white seeds, millions, billions of seeds equipped to rise with the slightest breeze and float to where more dandelions would grow. By the following spring, they had multiplied into a marauding horde that threatened the existence of the even sparser lawn.

Over the following decades I became inured to the lure of wildness in a garden, categorically rejecting egalitarianism. All plants are not created equal, and they don't have equal rights to reproduce. Contrary to the popular definition of weeds as a plant in the wrong place, or one that is more successful, our common weeds were imported from Europe by early settlers in a misguided effort to reproduce the landscape they had left behind. With no natural enemies in their new home, these foreigners continue to threaten the very survival of the natives.

The mustard was not merely out of place. It was a plundering invader with astounding reproductive success, the Genghis Khan of the natural world.

We waged the first battle the first spring we owned the property. Days in the sun, yanking out the rough stalks. Spreading them out on the driveway. Driving over them muttering curses. Then peeing over them repeatedly. (This was done not for botanical reasons but as a final, irremediable insult.) Leaving them to freeze over the winter. Having used up everything in our arsenal, the Vermont winter, we reasoned, would finish the job, as the Russian winter had defeated Napoleon's, then Hitler's armies.

But we were dealing with a superweed, a weed on steroids. Neither winter nor urine, hideous curses nor the weight of cars killed it. By early April, the undead hordes had covered the driveway with spiny stems and bursting buds. The few that had escaped our focused weeding in the nearby fields had multiplied, forming undulating mustard swaths amid the rich green. And emissaries of evil intent had been sent into far-flung areas.

There were many, many nay-sayers who, gazing at the golden fingers that reached into the farthest fields, insisted that mine was a futile effort.

"Impossible," they said. "Just look at how many there are!"

"You've really lost it up here on this lonely hill," noted a close friend who felt no need to be polite.

"They're biennial, you know, they'll lie dormant one year and reappear the next," warned another who fancied herself an expert because she was an outdoor educator.

"Why not just leave them, they look pretty," suggested some who knew nothing about the malevolence that emanated from those bright bobbing heads.

"If you can't beat them, eat them!" was Daniela's solution. She claimed they were delicious, like spinach only tastier, but the depth of my antipathy would make it impossible to digest them. No one understood that this was a war to the death. I could not lose. I would rather die of sunstroke than from the hatred that would surely consume me with curdling bitterness. The mustards and I could not inhabit the same hill. Either they or I would have to go, and I was staying.

Ted was willing to "help," but this was my project. He simply didn't share my intense loathing. An hour or so a day was his limit for this activity, which consisted of moving very slowly in a stooped position in the hot sun while yanking each plant up by the roots, then walking them to a pile of monsters. The piles were then moved to one central pile that grew into a small hill, which seemingly dead, contained the seeds of a future surge. Would they end in fire or ice? Ice had failed; fire was next on the agenda.

The annual war begins every year in early May and lasts through July. By then, I can spot a lone plant fifty feet away, even one slyly hiding in the towering grass. A section of stem, a bud are enough to send me crashing through the timothy and clover, barefoot and in shorts, stepping on who knows how many mice and snakes, lost in the pursuit to the death of the enemy.

Once, on a slow, after dinner walk in Palm Springs where we were visiting friends, I rushed across the wide boulevard and stood transfixed, my fingers wrapped around the chain link fence, knuckles white, lips open in a silent scream. There, in an empty lot in this foreign climate grew clumps of garlic mustard, the very same ones! They were stalking me! Showing up here, in the desert of all places, winking their yellow smile, torturing me! The friends watched me silently from across the road while Ted tried to explain, keeping his voice low. To their everlasting credit, they didn't question my behavior, at least not much.

Another spring. I gaze with joy at the grass, growing thick with the greening rains, the deep roots nourishing the regenerating surge. But I know better; it's simply too early for the outlaws.

The Mustard War has been dragging on for almost as long as we've been in Afghanistan. The enemy is losing its early momentum. Local pockets of resistance still pop up throughout the growing season, and in most of the original battlegrounds. But its numbers continue to shrink, and its vigor is not what it was. There are still many battles to be fought and days of crouching and yanking ahead, of dripping sweat and aching arms. But I am working on a victory flag that I will unfurl and fly from the rooftop. Soon.

FINISH LINE

When the house looked finished but still wasn't, we walked our meager belongings through shin-deep snow down from the cabin, where we had been spending more and more time as our commitment to work was winding down, and into the house. We could now sleep on blow-up mattresses on warm floors and revel in the indoor toilets. But the dust overwhelmed the aroma of new wood and settled overnight on the sleeping bags, on hair and in nostrils. We retreated back to the cabin, grateful for the clean smell of wood burning in the stove.

Only minor work remained, we told ourselves, work that couldn't possibly take the months Michael predicted. But those details and that qualifying "nearly" turned out to be rather major projects, including a few intractable challenges.

For one, the only way upstairs, which consisted of our bedroom, bathroom and a landing that was to be Ted's office, was by climbing a ladder. Once upstairs, the triangular bathtub occupied the bedroom. All the doors, including the front door, were missing. Lights still consisted of bare bulbs hanging from wires. And neither of the two porches was finished.

"You are not done," Michael repeated daily.

"*I* am not done?"

"I can't be done till *you* are done."

He was right. I wasn't done. Not with the decisions nor with the searches. Open or closed staircase? An open staircase creates the illusion of more space and light. But the space underneath it is wasted. What about the treads, Michael asked. What about them, I inquired. I had never considered that treads and risers can be made in any size. Isn't there a standard size then? Not really. For several days I measured the treads and risers of stairs -- ours, neighbors', friends', offices' and (secretly) a bank's and a movie theater's.

The large wasteful bathtub was another worry. Once filled, I'd need to spend a good portion of a day in it to justify the cost of the hot water. Therefore, it would be nice to look out the windows that made up the bathroom walls. To do that, the tub would have to be some four feet off the floor, directly below the windows. There was no shortage of ideas, design magazines being full of fascinating bathrooms with marble steps leading to enormous tubs, but both our bathroom and budget were too small. In the end, the carpenters built a platform that enclosed the tub, and finished it off with bead-board. A marine ladder would get me up and down safely.

The front door turned out to be a trial. Michael threatened to remove his crew and machinery, leaving the house open to the elements. I promised that we'd find a door in time. There are, after all, hundreds of doors made by dozens of companies.

Why should a door create such a fuss? Just get a door, any style, said Ted, insisting he no longer cared. But the design called for a pair of French doors, which would provide the only downstairs view to the north and the woods. Not your usual entry door, but not unheard of either. However, no ready-made door fit into the cut the architect designed, a cut already made and now covered with vivid blue plastic. Ultimately, with some fancy carpentry work, the crew was able to amend the opening and install the simple doors with cut glass that I knew the house craved.

The screened porch should have been straightforward. A small room off the living room with screens for walls. A floor of poured concrete, cut into large squares of golden brown, was complete. So was the ceiling, a lovely high ceiling of pine. So what was the problem?

"No problem," Michael responded. When several long moments passed in silent staring into space, I knew from months of experience that there was a zinger to come.

"As long as you're willing to pay for custom-made windows and screens."

We were not. Willing or able.

"Or, we can install regular windows that open and close instead of the screen/window combination."

He already knew we didn't want windows. This was to be an open porch. Windows made it a room. Something had to be done. Those somethings always involved compromise. So we compromised on walls that came up higher and lower. It turned out to be a proper and beautiful screened porch.

But there was another porch on the other side of the living room, an open twin of the screened porch, held up by two posts. These were not to be just any posts; these posts would define the porch and would be visible from the entrance. They had to make a statement. Since the architect looked blank every time I raised the issue of posts, it was now up to me to find these architectural elements, which in the end turned out to be not a pair but two groups of three slender columns, each with a "root" spreading onto the floor. The metal bands that were to tie the roots to the columns are still waiting to happen.

Another retaining column was needed between the kitchen and dining area. One would look odd, I insisted. But that's what the plan showed, Michael pointed out. If we wanted two, he could do that. It would cost more. How much more? Well, that depended on the kind of columns we wanted. We didn't know what we wanted. He knew that perfectly well. How about using some of the fallen trees in the woods, peeling the trunks and turning them into rustic columns? Michael hates rustic. He threatened us with armies of wood-boring insects that would in no time dismantle our new house. We were on the verge of an argument. We told him to make "nice" columns, two of them please.

The argument we couldn't avoid was over the kitchen. It was beautiful, even the handles, another item I was too exhausted to choose properly. When the books were presented, each showing a few hundred handles, I pushed them away.

"Show me three you like," I asked the store's designer.

"You don't want to do that! You want to make sure it's what *you* like."

"No, I really want to do that. I can't look through these," I said, waving in distress at the books.

So she showed me three and I picked one, and I continue to like them very much.

The issue with the kitchen was a new item that popped up in one of the regular bills. It was for kitchen installation.

"It took time," Michael noted, and stopped, wrongly assuming that this was sufficient explanation.

"Have you ever built a house without installing a kitchen?" I asked.

He repeated his first statement.

"It wasn't on the proposal as a separate item," Ted insisted. "It's a given that a kitchen would have to be installed."

"It didn't install itself, it took my guys time to do it," Michael responded obtusely.

Michael is far from obtuse, so we knew we had him. He had forgotten to list it. It was unfair to surprise us with yet another expense at such a late stage. It was also unfair to not pay him for his time.

The television presented the insurmountable challenge that threatened to ravage the exemplary partnership Ted and I had through great effort and admirable maturity maintained through all the months of construction.

Television doesn't play a major part in our lives but we do have one. And we happened to have a new, large, flat-screen one that had just recently replaced the set that had finally died in the dank basement where for twenty years it had struggled to perform its duties. This new purchase was for the new house, where its elegant lines and slim profile would fit on the smallest wall.

The first alarm came with Michael's early morning call.

"Where do you want us to mount the hardware for the TV?"

A simple question, with an obvious answer.

"In the living room."

"OK, but where? The only wall is the one where we're installing lights for your large painting over the sofa. Do you want the TV there instead? Then you don't need the lights."

"No, of course not. The sofa has to go somewhere, right?"

"There's no other wall."

"Really? That can't be."

But it could. And it was. The layout was imprinted in my brain. There was no other wall. Except for the wall behind the sofa, there was no wall in the living area. There was no wall in the guest bedrooms either. They all consisted of windows or closets. Ditto for our bedroom. We spent an afternoon the following weekend walking around, considering every unlikely possibility. There was a narrow space in the bedroom upstairs, but that would mean just one chest for the two of us. We could put it under the stairs in the hall, but where would we sit? We did this on-site research separately, because our feelings were rapidly morphing from calm to hot and angry. Finally we bumped into each other in the living room, where we had started.

"You finally got the house you always wanted. A glass house!" Ted was fairly sputtering.

"But isn't it wonderful to have all these windows?" I insisted, turning in a wide arc, my arms embracing the outdoors. "There is virtually no difference between being indoors and out."

This was not a convenient defense. But I was ecstatic at the flood of light, at the world that came into the house with minor interruptions of just enough wall in the corners to hold the glass.

"Yes, yes, I know. But I warned you and warned you that there were no walls!"

"You did not! You said there were too many windows!"

"Same thing. Too many windows mean not enough walls!"

"It's not the same thing at all! You never even mentioned walls! You only mention them now because of the TV!" I was not going to be defeated by lack of accuracy.

The argument devolved into straight out yelling, and continued to grow in volume due to a lack of objects to bang since the house was still blissfully empty.

That night, we slept in separate rooms, each to his or her own sleeping bag. In the morning, we decided to exchange the television for a smaller one and build a small wall between the hall and living room to hang it on.

"And let's enjoy the windows," I said.

"In peace, if we can," Ted added as we walked out into the early sun.

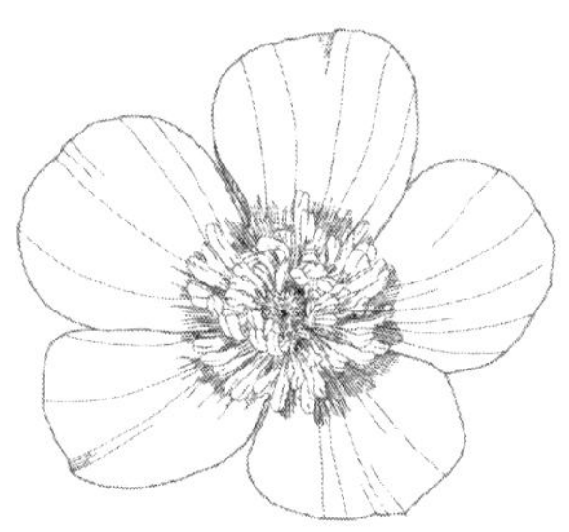

Stillness

Sitting still is no easy thing for me.

I once saw a photo of a woman with a large-brimmed hat sitting in a field. On the hat brim sat a couple of birds, and another bird sat in her open palm, and the bird and the woman were looking at each other. The caption explained that she spends hours a day sitting perfectly still in that same spot, so the birds learned to see her as part of the scenery.

I admire this woman. Clearly, she has entered a universe beyond the fidgety one I inhabit. Patience, as family and good friends have repeatedly pointed out, is not among my virtues. I fill every moment with activity. To sit still doing nothing is a rare occurrence; it may happen some evenings for the minutes when I watch the sun before it drops behind the Adirondacks. But that's hardly doing nothing. And even during those already full moments, I find myself compiling mental lists and schedules. Or searching for words, words, words to capture the splendor.

How I wish I could, just once, be purged of the torrent of words! Be perfectly still, not drumming fingers on the table or running them through hair or noticing the garden-chipped nails. To neither plan nor remember.

I will do it. Now.

I place a chair in the field. The faded lumpy cushion too. Comfort is important. But no books, no binoculars, no sweater, no water. Nothing for my hands to take up or distract my eyes.

I sit, and the heavy grass heads rise above me. I am embraced in a tight circle of green sunlight. I place my hands on the armrests and wait for the buzz in my head to cease. I need to be open to voices other than my own. I will now watch the buttercup at work, I tell myself, then silence the thought. Words rushing in are an intrusion. I must stop trying to lasso the great mystery of the buttercup with words.

There is deep silence in the pulsing hum. I close my eyes and wait for the light and air to pour through my head and fill me as it fills the buttercup. I am daring myself to just be. To just linger in these moments, to not remember the moments just passed in frustration at not finding the right word among the millions ricocheting in my brain. To ignore the moments to come. The weeds in the vegetable boxes, propelling powerful stems toward the sun. The backseat stuffed with chores. My neighbor's organic but skinny chicken that should be marinating. Move beyond the mad drive to do, to schedule, to accomplish. Stop drifting into memories and expectations.

The claims on my time and compassion are too many. Lost in my blessed existence, I feel defenseless in the rush of misery that comes at me from every corner of the world. I could do more.

Stop being jerked about by guilt. These moments and all the others will slip away and be lost.

The ties of guilt and duty begin to slacken. For a long spell I sit in a wakeful hush, finally lingering in the present. A ruffle of wind feathers my ankles, but no sound follows. That was a thought, worthless, mundane. Silence, I tell myself.

My eye alights on something bright in the grass – the chitinous shell of an insect caught in a spiderweb. It's still alive, and one tiny leg curls rhythmically. The web hangs between blades of grass. My eye traces the geometric perfection of its construction. I consider that the silk in the web is stronger than a steel thread of the same thickness.

Stop, stop. The spaces in my head are filled with such trivia. How can anything worthwhile fit into what is, after all, a finite space? I shut my mind to thought.

Now I bask in the warmth again. Under closed eyelids I record the dance of light. I shrug off time and linger in the sweetness.

There is life raging under my feet in the earth, and in every shoot of weaving grass coursing with wild energy, and above too, where birds are wheeling and weaving drunkenly in the sun-warmed air. The same silent energy could pour through me too -- if I let it. I drift again and my ears fill with the pulse of a nearby cicada. My breath mingles with the breeze and the odor of the soil. It is rich with life and death, with fallen insects mingling with last year's grass and spring's flowers in a ferment of decay.

Decay. The web will decay and the spider that spun it, along with whatever remains of its prey. Memories return, a cloying sadness for all the remembered spiderwebs of long ago, for all the unreturning childhood summers. Then a sharp sadness for all the unreturning dead, and for the murdered I never knew. Sitting on this flowery earth, I am drowning in sadness.

I can't. I can't let this thought go. I can't let go my crowded self. All the clamoring people who live inside me, whose only proof of existence is inside me, who will die their final death when I die. For now, they too deserve to sit with me here, to walk the fields, to see the flower heads wave, to have this glistening air fill them.

Between Two Lives

My eyes are fixed in a hard stare, unblinking, drying out on the unlit road, one white-knuckled hand grasping the wheel while the other rummages in the remains of my dinner. A whole basket of fried chicken and shrimp, French fries and diet soda, topped off with a sugar cone filled with Death-by-Chocolate ice cream, more bad food than I consume in a month. Every lurch threatens to send the toaster oven and microwave balanced on the boxes on the back seat crashing into my head. Worse, the predicted thunderstorm is about to unleash its fury, tardy but undiminished.

I left work early but still too late. Before I left the house, I interviewed one last real estate agent and hired her. Caught in the long-predicted real estate bust of 2008 and the unpredicted Great Recession, our old house remained unsold after six months on the market despite the greatly reduced price. It was the woods and curvy roads, the lack of sidewalks and streetlights, the very things that made the neighborhood so special to us, that buyers didn't like!

I left Ted filling box after box with stuff he was carrying down from the attic, a section of the house we had somehow forgotten about. The boxes were bursting with memorabilia from our children's school days, from old jobs, from plays, parties and weddings attended, my yellowed wedding dress, millennium sunglasses with "2000" making up the nose piece, antique silver stored for a friend and truly forgotten by both of us, burnt-orange carpet remnants from 1979, college diplomas never framed, urine-colored newspaper clips with my by-line, electric space heaters and window air conditioners. A journey in time we'd have to take another time. Because I had finished packing my old car, and despite Ted's logical warnings about my poor driving ability in general and the unimaginably poor driving I will do for two hundred miles in the dark and exhausted, I was on my way. He would follow in the morning.

I had waited a decade for this day. My new life would start not the following day but that night, when I'd go to sleep on our new mattress in our new house in the fields I had named Prairie Hill, a name my children found pretentious but which I still believe fits perfectly.

It had been my last day in the office. Every two or three weeks I would return for a day, but I would by then be a minor celebrity and later just an ordinary visitor. The office, the organization, its people, would become peripheral, the politics and intrigues would rapidly lose their hold. The void, if any, would be saturated with the new life that was waiting at the end of the proverbial road. Neither dark nor distance, storm nor exhaustion were going to keep me from even a single night of this new life. Fueled by a large mug of coffee, I left with visions of sinking into sleep in the unspoiled dark and waking to the sun topping Birdseye.

At 2 a.m., pursued by wild wind and stabbing lightning, I dashed into the house. No memory of sinking into the mattress or admiring the dark. Only immense relief at having survived the trip. Of having arrived.

When Ted pulled up in late afternoon, he found me amid pyramids of pulled wild mustard. Immensely grateful to finally be outdoors, he volunteered to weed with me. We built more, even taller pyramids. Then we hauled in boxes of books and children's artwork, stacks of dishes and bags of groceries. I made dinner with swordfish, dilled potatoes, and kale, a celebration. We ate it outside on folding chairs. Then, with the sun still above the Adirondacks, crawled onto the mattress for chocolate and champagne. In the morning, I tried out my new life by going back to bed after coffee, and watched yesterday's clouds blowing in huge cargoes across Birdseye and out to sea, somewhere in Maine.

For weeks after, we were driving, and living, between the past and the future.

The furniture was left in the old house, waiting for the house to be sold. In the new house, we constructed a table from sawhorses and a plank covered with a bright cloth, surrounded by folding chairs. Inflatable mattresses served as sofas. Our few clothes sat on closet floors, since these lacked shelves or racks. Only the kitchen and bathroom were stocked and usable.

None of this mattered. It was July, and the days spun out, interminable. We woke early and lived in a blaze of sun. We worked inside and out, with breaks for swims and occasional bike rides. Each time we drove up and saw the house rise at the top, we were shocked anew. We had not yet developed the habit of thinking of it, and of this whole hill as ours. That would take months, a full year.

The grass seeds we scattered over barely prepared ground sprouted and covered the graybrown earth with a thin pale coat. Then the fields moved in, clover and harsh orchard grass, and the lawn grew thick and dark. By the end of the month it needed regular mowing, and Ted took up his favorite chore: riding the old tractor noisily up the driveway and spending an hour mowing concentric circles until he reached the middle of the semi circular lawn. Then he would get off the tractor, remove the ludicrously huge red ear protectors, and gaze contentedly at his handiwork. Within four days he'd marvel at the rate of growth, excited at the next rapidly approaching tractoring experience. I weeded, planted, set up an office in the cabin, lined kitchen drawers. We put up a mailbox and ordered the local paper, which we read assiduously, intent on learning the issues in our new state. We both dusted, daily, hourly. The dust of construction covered and recovered every surface, wandering in gossamer curtains in the empty house. I too wandered from task to task, rejoicing in the unimpeded space.

I never wanted furniture again.

Each day we discovered some new delight. The high sun of summer lit the front porch first. Before six, we could sit there with coffee, sunwashed. It was also the best place to sit out rain and wind, since summer winds rarely came from the north. The kitchen island could accommodate two stools at one end and still leave plenty of room for baking multiple breads and cakes. From the bedroom windows, horses and cows were visible on a hillside directly across. The screened porch made for an old-fashioned sleeping porch – as long as the wind didn't blow the sheets off.

Every week or two we drove back to the old house, where we mowed and trimmed and weeded and packed up more stuff. Still filled with our furniture, and with every sharply detailed memory of our children, with their friends' maturing faces at the door, with extended family gatherings, with the last time each of our parents had sat at the dining room table, the house seemed strangely hollow. Its air, empty of daily life, was filled with the guilt I felt toward this once loved and now dreaded house. I returned alone one more time on a warm September day intending to spend the night. But the vacant chill drove me to seek refuge at a friend's home. This, I thought, must be how a divorce feels. A love flourished and gave life, and then it moved on, leaving an empty shell.

Then there was the "stuff." Piles, heaps, stacks, hoards, profusions, amassments of accumulated objects I didn't need, and many I didn't know I had. Platters and trays, vases and wrong-sized sheets, forgotten cacti and useless gadgets, non working flashlights, storage containers and lids that didn't match, outdated clothes and shoes and shrunken scarves and ancient skis, a dozen candleholders and two dozen mugs, pretty but unused teacups and saucers, the chandelier in our first apartment on which we paid a year of installments, endless pens, trimmers, rusted garden implements, term papers, dissertations, a fishing vest! We didn't even know anyone who fished! And books, books, books.

All these possessions were mortifying to someone who prides herself on living simply and abhorring clutter. Here was unmistakable, three-dimensional proof of our wasteful lifestyle. If we had all this junk, what did the average American, for whom shopping was a national pastime and a requirement for citizenship, accumulate in twenty-nine years?

Westchester is a mostly wealthy area. We tried to sell, then give away the good items and furniture. Unsuccessful, the amassment moved to the curb where it was piled into three small mountains that reached up the oak trunks. Ultimately, desperate to be rid of the reminders of our shocking profligacy, we paid the Salvation Army for their removal. The last to go was a large, ugly and hated corn plant that had been passed down to me from my father's aunt, who had had it most of her life until she moved to a nursing home at age ninety-seven. I left it on the compost pile near the woods, wishing it a rewarding life as rich humus.

After the house was finally sold in the middle of the worst housing slump in decades (so much for our careful financial planning), I reluctantly agreed to move the little furniture that remained. I had developed great appreciation for the spaciousness of an unfurnished house. I argued that with shelves in the closet, we could give up the bedroom chests. All I wanted was the comfortable sofa and the dining table and chairs, folding chairs having proven discouraging to long dinners. Ted's saner mind prevailed, and the chests arrived along with the rest of our minimal furniture. During the following year, I gave away every platter and bowl and vase that well-meaning guests brought to warm our new home. They couldn't know I like the house cold. It has the Zen quality I've always craved. Its empty corners and bare surfaces are a balm. Unimpeded, the outdoors pours in. The pulsing green or glittering white, the truncated call of flying geese, a fat bee, a leaping fox, apple blossoms, row on row of autumn mountains, the mercurial sky.

Good Riddance

Along with possessions, I've been trying to rid myself of behaviors, specifically those that create conflict with our new community. Success has been slow and spotty. I continue to be too demanding of myself and others, and I have to remind myself on each occasion to not judge people hastily. I struggle to bury these traits under the accumulating changes being wrought in us. Living alone on this hill, exposed by turns to nature's coddling and its violence, is precipitating much of the change. Vermont's people are also forcing us to reconsider long-held values and learn new ways of being part of the social fabric.

In Vermont, much of the time, you can't tell a book by its cover. Its people don't fit into covers, no matter how roomy, oddly-shaped, elastic.

There's the truck driver who earned a philosophy degree from one of the Ivies. The seamstress was a fine arts major. The quiet medical technician regularly leaves her tiny house to scuba dive in the world's remotest waters. The retired high-school teacher stacks boxes in a mail-order warehouse so he can live in Vermont and is very happy, thank you. The former corporate executive raises llamas on an uphill farm and sells Christmas decorations fashioned from their wool. A friend with two advanced degrees sews potholders to sell at craft shows. And the erudite farmers compose newsletters that between recipes for sautéed chard and stir-fried radishes explore the philosophy of local production and its impact on the world's future.

Out for a short hike on a late fall afternoon, I met a very old man in an even older parka walking toward me slowly, a crooked stick in each hand. We greeted each other. I wondered if his teary eyes and red nose meant he was cold. And that ancient, huge jacket. Was he, could he possibly be homeless, camping out here? What would happen to him in the winter? Searching for an unobtrusive way to determine if he needed help, I engaged him in conversation. Since I was somewhat lost, as I am on every hike, getting directions was the obvious opener. In a strong voice, the old man pointed the way, including shortcuts and lookout points not to be missed. Impressed, I carried on the exchange, learning that he was the undisputed owner of all those hundreds of acres of fields, cliffs and streams and lived in the tiny brown house I had passed at the entrance.

This meeting did more than confirm Vermonter's refreshing attitude toward displays of wealth. It began to clear the fog surrounding the vanishing contractors. It explained why they were friendly and pleasant but quickly chose not to even try to get a crack at building our house. Living in a small state with an even smaller population, people know each other or know of each other and are therefore friendly. This was not the case before we moved here when we found them frustratingly uncommunicative, but then we weren't living here. It was, I realized, not the size or the shape or even the engineering elements that made the house "green"; it was us, just as we suspected. These people may have been folksy but they were also intelligent, and they understood that we would bring our big-city attitudes to the project. We'd demand professionalism, an aesthetic quality bordering on perfection, and a business attitude that would broach no waste of time. It's how we were used to functioning because that's what our environment demanded of us. And they knew we were sure to demand it of them. They also knew this was not their style and why should they try to change it for us?

Vermonters are on the whole well read thanks to the long winters, well educated thanks to an across-the-board commitment to education, well informed, and politically progressive. They are ingenious, finding imaginative ways to implement the ethic of fixing and reusing whatever is around. Ted raised $300 for the library at the town-wide yard sale with out-of-date dental tools that he sold for a dollar a piece. Hearing the inventive uses for these tools – from needlecrafts to auto repairs – was instructive.

This devotion to home-based innovation, coupled with Vermonters' relative poverty, may account for the dismal shopping opportunities the state offers. Anything less than a decade old is deemed fashionable. Most of the time, I've learned to enjoy not being judged by my bag and shoes. I'm happy I can let my hair go naturally "silver" without getting critical stares. But I still refuse to wear fleece, Vermonters' three- season garment of choice.

Among Vermonters' unconventional aspects is their attitude toward careers. Work of any kind is only a means to an end. And the end is very modest: a basic shelter in a pretty location, a reliable vehicle, a bicycle, canoe, snowshoes, fresh local produce. Time for hunting is another requirement for many. Work is neither honorable, nor respectable, nor important. It just is. It's rarely discussed and never used to establish rank. It's what you do to live, and once you have enough to live on, it's sufficient. Working more to earn more or growing a business for greater prestige and income are generally not considered. Just enough is enough.

This is an excellent attitude that meshes perfectly with the state's economy, which is small and likely to remain so. With a slowly declining population of just six hundred and twenty thousand people – about a third less than suburban Westchester County –- and environmental restrictions that hamper large development of any kind, there are few jobs with growth potential. Young people leave, then often return when they have families, wanting to raise their children here. Others forego professional success in return for all the intangibles the state offers.

Unable to overcome decades of conditioning in Manhattan's hyper-competitive career hothouse, I am often lost. Unable to slap on easy labels, I am learning to let people reveal themselves, slowly. I'm learning to speak more slowly, to listen better, to not fill the silent spaces that punctuate conversation, to ask for the other's opinion and offer mine only when asked.

Age discrimination is another bad habit I've discarded. With so few people around, one cannot socialize only with one's age group. People's friends come in all ages and are chosen based on criteria other than age. It's inspiring to see how vital an octogenarian can be or how much people much younger than me can know about things I know little about, from vegetable growing to community organizing. This diversity helps make up a bit for the racial diversity that makes New York so rich and which is so absent here.

People in Vermont know each other. Far fewer than six degrees of separation exist between any two residents. Because the state is actually a sprawling city, with the interdependence and familiarity a city implies.

Out biking one morning, we stopped on the steps of a neighboring town's library to check the map. The librarian came out to see if we needed help. We didn't, but we had a short chat about the Friends of the Library group in our town. The following afternoon, stopping at my town's library, the librarian repeated our conversation verbatim.

"Is anything wrong?" she inquired, seeing my dumbfounded expression.

"No, nothing, I just can't believe this non-news traveled so far so fast!" I answered.

"Oh, well, everyone knows everyone here, you know."

It's something I try to remember before any thought that forms in my brain escapes my lips. Secrecy and anonymity are not options here. Still, the high degree of tolerance for the right to be eccentric, even woefully misguided, makes life here for "direct" people like me possible.

The knowing goes both ways. We are as known as we know. The UPS driver decided long ago that it was easier to drop off our packages at Ted's office in the village than drive up our hill. Sometimes, he finds an even better shortcut.

"I was waiting in the doctor's office when suddenly I hear this booming, familiar voice," Ted's assistant recounted to me the other day. "It was the UPS driver. He said he was so glad to see me because he had a package for the people on the hill and wanted to leave it with me. In the waiting room! He was about to run to his truck when I stopped him. I told him he really should deliver it to you directly, since I only work every other day. Deliver it to the address on the label, I said."

He was taken aback, she reported. Of course! Why, he wanted to know, when he could just give it to her right there? What did the address on the label have to do with the happy coincidence of them meeting just when he had a package for us, saving even the short trip to Ted's office?

So what did he do? Did he bring me the book I had been waiting for? Of course not. Two days later he dropped it off at the office, for me to pick up. I could complain, but what will that do to the goodwill I'm trying to build among all the people who know me, or know of me through others, or will soon know me? And how likely am I to succeed in changing the prevailing attitude? A few years ago, I might have tried. Now I know better.

This newfound patience was sorely tested as I was being prepped for one of those routine and exceptionally unpleasant medical exams. Chatting me up in a vain attempt to make me relax, the nurse noted the book I was holding and asked if I liked to read. No, I wanted to say, I carry books everywhere I go, on my head, as an exercise in good posture.

Here, I thought, was another opportunity to show that I have learned how to get along in Vermont. Being unfriendly is simply not an option. People who know each other are friendly to each other, and while we two didn't know each other, the assumption was that henceforth we would. Still, I deliberately chose to behave as I would have in a Manhattan clinic.

The nurse, however, was not to be put off. She proceeded to questions about my work. "Write," I said, and stopped, determined to say not another word. But this was enough information for the nurse to make an astounding connection.

"That's so interesting!" she enthused. "Just last week, I had another woman, also a writer, in this, in this bed!"

This can't be right, I thought. What about privacy? Professional discretion?

She continued describing the other writer's past and current professional life. After the second item in her CV I knew exactly who had undergone the same test a week ago. I was planning my opening sentence when I would call her to report what I learned. This amused me for a while, until a new thought struck me, which I had no time to explore before I was put out.

Who, lying in this bed next week would be hearing about my test and calling *me* for a good laugh?

When people here say that virtually everyone knows everyone else, they're barely exaggerating. Within certain parameters, that is. The Northeast Kingdom is a separate, remote world, even more sparsely populated than the rest of the state and some ten degrees colder on average than the "Banana Belt" down by us. In the first four years we lived in Vermont, we had no occasion to go there, but were finally drawn by its wild beauty. Then there is Burlington, a major metropolis by Vermont standards. About a third of state residents live in and around the city, forming their own separate sphere of "urban" Vermont. That leaves about three hundred and fifty thousand in the rest of the state, inhabiting nearly ten thousand square miles or about a third of the land area, with an average state density of sixty-seven people per square mile.

So it's not surprising that we're constantly meeting people we know.

Not only in the village but at concerts, the farmer's market, the co-op, fundraisers, at one or the other of two summer theaters, at restaurants, bookstores and at a busy calendar of community events. We've met and chatted informally with the lone Vermont representative to Congress and with the governor several times. Of course, we meet the people who frequent the same places we do, so this is a largely self-selective process.

The surprise is that not only Ted, who is a thoroughly social animal, but I too enjoy knowing and being known. Being greeted by name at every stop in the village is an unexpected pleasure. Finding groups of acquaintances ready to share their spot on the green at summer concerts elevates the quality of the music several rungs. Getting involved in the community and in causes is especially gratifying, since it takes relatively little money to make a noticeable difference. In the end, we miss the world-class culture of New York City much less than we expected. It can't hold a candle to the pleasure generated by close interaction with the sincere, intelligent people we are learning to appreciate. Plus, we tell our New York friends, culture is available all the time, from excellent music to professional theater to big-screen classic movies. Sure, it's on a smaller scale. But there is the added pleasure of knowing that so many people we know are enjoying the same words or music. There is always so much to talk about.

Still, we warn our friends in New York, and anyone contemplating a move. "Don't move unless you must." Or unless you want to live your dream, I add silently. The gap left by the people with whom we've gone to school, raised children, worked daily for years is real. There are no substitutes for friendships formed through years of sharing the experiences that define our lives. So don't move because you found a better climate or a state with lower taxes. Stay where you are. You will miss the sun much less than lifelong friends.

The Language of Stones

Opening the kitchen door onto mud, rocks and weeds was a daily reminder that even though Michael and his men and machines were gone, construction was not quite over. We needed something other than mud to sit on to watch the summer sunsets and walk on to the outdoor shower.

Since we live in Slate Valley, a slate patio seemed the obvious choice, and one we could possibly build ourselves. But after looking into the carefully laid multiple layers of sand and crushed rock that preceded the laying of stones, we decided, despite my affinity to stones, that this was a project best left to professionals.

I was inspired by a trip to Ireland where I saw hundreds of miles of stone walls, paths, terraces and steps. I was imagining something similar, with huge uneven stones that spoke of time and of a history we didn't have. If not that, at least a freeform creation in stone, inspired by the Adirondacks whose tapered peaks would gleam over the patio distantly.

The stone artist came from an unlikely source: the program guide to the Vermont Symphony Orchestra. The placement and the tasteful ad featuring a magnificent stone wall were powerful endorsement. I called and received more photos of his work, all impressive. After getting a few references, we got together.

The stone artist, it turned out, was quite young, and so was his partner, who was also his girlfriend. And while he was not a music patron, his mother was, which to my desperate mind was nearly as good. We wanted the patio built before the end of summer, when we planned a large family party to celebrate our fortieth anniversary and a number of significant birthdays.

"We were thinking of a freeform design with uneven stones," I began. "About from here to here and reaching out toward the mountains."

The stone artist and his girlfriend nodded in agreement, but remained silent.

"How large do *you* see it?" Ted asked, seeking specificity.

"Hard to know at this point. The stones will tell us."

This answer was not at all clear to me, but I was willing to continue the conversation, with a fresh start.

"We saw this gorgeous stone terrace in Ireland with a planter for herbs in the middle," I began, whipping out the photos.

"That might work, but it really depends on the stones."

"So will it stretch from that corner to this one?" Ted persisted, stuck on the size. I shot him a look, which he ignored.

"Hard to know, but probably, depending on the stones."

"Well, when will you and we know?"

"After we start laying out the stones."

"But won't it be too late then? What if we don't like the shape or size?

"The stones won't let us make a mistake."

At this, Ted did finally look at me. It was a look I knew well, filled with silent warnings. It was my turn to ignore him. I was intrigued with this new concept of the stones having a decision-making capacity. Somewhat New Age maybe, but then they were the artists. We hadn't dealt with stones on such an intimate level and therefore lacked the intuitive understanding these people had.

"The stones speak to you?" Ted inquired in an even tone. I was mortified. But the stone artists must have been used to this line of obtuse questioning and remained unflappable.

"In a way."

This stopped Ted from further questioning. Later he defended his silence by saying he felt ill equipped to argue with such insanity, but I was sure he could see that these artists were functioning on a different plane.

Still, he was, surprisingly, not averse to hiring them, provided we could supervise the construction on a daily basis. Also -- and this was a stumbling block until I explained that this is how Ted likes to set things up but he's by no means a rigid, irrational person -- to have the right to fire them at any time and pay only for work done.

They picked out the stones, which I went to examine at a local dealer. There they were, stacked upright, on three pallets. What I was supposed to look at I had no idea. They were huge, thick, and slate colored. I said I liked them very much, trying to be encouraging and show confidence in their ability.

For the first few days, the work involved pouring and flattening many layers of sand and gravel. On the following Monday, they finally carried a stone, then another and a third to the base. She gave the instructions, and they moved and positioned and repositioned each one. By early afternoon, the end of their workday, they had fitted four stones in place, a jigsaw puzzle in the making. It looked promising. I went and stood on the stones and gazed from them to the horizon and back. It looked very much like the germ of a patio.

The next morning, I went out and stood on the stones again, coffee mug in hand. I drank the whole cup, waiting for the caffeine to kick in and rev up my concentration. I wanted to be focused, open to the stones. I put the mug down and walked over to the pallet. I pushed a smallish one off and nudged it near the embryonic patio. It didn't fit. No matter which direction I pushed it in. I tried with another, larger stone, and with a third even larger one that I dragged along walking backward, tripping on the first one I left in the way and landing on my coccyx, which although painful, was better than my skull. It still didn't fit. I had to face it. The stones didn't speak to me. Not that morning, nor on any other day.

Meanwhile, the patio grew, expanding unevenly in various directions, ungainly and strange.

"Where will the herb planter go?" I asked one day when the artists appeared less dour than usual.

"Out there," she indicated.

"But won't that be too far? I mean, the patio would then have to be enormous to wrap around it."

She gave me a pitying look.

"It will wrap around the patio, okay?"

"What will?"

"The planter. It will be out there and the patio will be here," she explained, her body rigid.

"Oh, but we agreed it would be in the middle! Or somewhere near the middle!"

"Yes, but the stones demanded that it be around the patio."

"When did they do that?"

This was not a ridiculous question. I really did want to know at what point the decision was made. Knowing this would lead to an understanding of this mysterious communication with the stones, a dialogue that shut me out. I love stones, and trees and birds, almost anything in nature, with the exception of exceptionally large slugs, howling coyotes and invasive plants, so I felt I had earned the privilege of having the stones talk to me too, or at least provide vague hints in whatever obscure means they chose. Even if I wasn't a stone artist.

He and she looked at each other. I kept my gaze steady on her.

"We can change it if you want, but we recommend having the planter wrap around the patio."

A good answer, since I too could now see that it would look better and leave us more room on the patio itself. Still, it was not the answer I sought. So I was not about to let them off the hook.

"We'll discuss it and let you know," I said.

"When?" she asked.

"After we consult with the stones."

When the patio was very near completion, with a week's worth of work left, the stone artists stopped showing up. After two attempts at coaxing them back, he showed up by himself. She never returned. It turned out it wasn't, after all, my sarcasm that kept them away; they had suddenly split up. After years of being a couple and business partners. Right in the middle of our project. With the house guests and party looming.

He promised it would be completed in time. He began arriving before brunch and staying beyond teatime. And he began consulting with us instead of the stones. Apparently, the stones became as recalcitrant with him as they had been with me. Were they talking only to her? Why not to him too? He was the stone artist, after all. It was puzzling.

It wasn't until the patio, both rough and smooth, planned and surprising, altogether beautiful, was indeed ready almost on schedule, that I understood. The stones. They spoke to two people at a time. Never to just one. I should have gotten Ted to join me in the conversation.

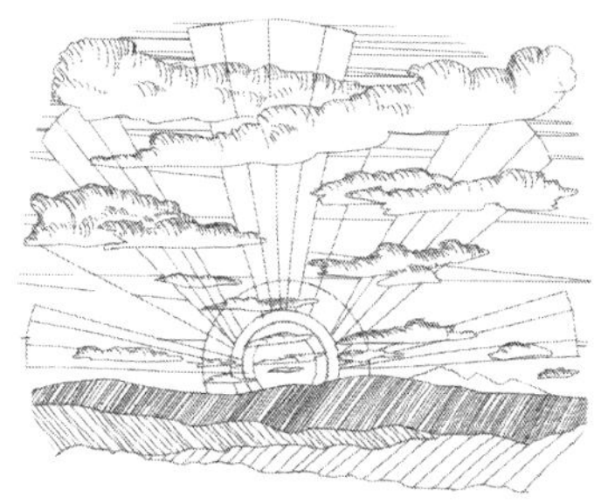

Sky

"This was a four or maybe, maybe a five."

"You think? It was a bit above average. Maybe a six."

"Nah. Just think of what we had Wednesday and we rated it seven."

"True. So let's give it a five."

"I'm now inclined toward a four."

"But look, more flames now. Look, they're all across, and deepening. Purple!"

"OK then, it's a five."

So go our conversations at the nightly skyshow.

No matter how many we witness, each sunset is different from all those that went before. Its location changes with the seasons. The lit clouds range across the color wheel, with infinite combinations. The sun itself may be any shade, from pale, moon yellow to blazing crimson. It may drop against clear aquatic blue, which rarely yields more than a rating of three, or against a multitude of billowing clouds, flaming the entire sky, reaching even the rare ten.

I forget yesterday's in the splendor of today's. I've learned to predict the level of the coming spectacle by the shape, size and location of the clouds. Clouds low on the horizon will cheat us of the final extravaganza.

Just above the horizon, they will serve as a canvas for luminous stacked bands of red, orange, yellow, violet, blue. A clear, empty sky is the least promising. The sun simply bows out without a curtain. Even a sky hidden beneath thick clouds offers more; after an entire day's absence, the sun often winks brilliantly from a shred in the clouds before it's extinguished for the night.

For a whole week one November, when we had already made peace with the bleak dimness that had descended, we were treated to a nightly show when the sun, crouching in a mantle of cumulus clouds, inflamed them into a fiery pageant. The scarlet ran down onto the dying fields.

In the end, words, even pigments are poor substitutes for this daily pageant, a spectacle painted with the light of the cosmos.

"You're pathetic," my daughter, then a teenager, pronounced. I confided that I spent most of each day looking forward to the best part: getting into bed.

I tried explaining.

"You know how great it feels to take off all your clothes, to slide under soft sheets. And this mattress! It feels like you're lying in the arms of a sumo wrestler, both softly cradling and muscularly supportive."

"Aha ..."

"You know how busy I am all day. And then to be released from all responsibilities and have time to read for no purpose other than pleasure."

"Aha ..."

"Really, if it were not a nightly event, if it took effort and cost money, this nightly bliss would be considered a rare luxury. It would be covered in magazines and on talk shows!"

She remained unmoved. "Yeah, but you're still pathetic," she pronounced with teenage arrogance.

My yearning for bedtime hasn't diminished in the intervening years. Yet I fritter away many minutes standing by the window, staring into the dark. Sometimes, in any season, I walk out into the night. Stepping barefoot into grass my feet know takes courage. Snakes, worms, voles, skunks, possums, spiders, fireflies, beetles, fantastically large moths, all content to ignore me in daylight may not be at night. Never have any crossed my path, and yet, could they be as disoriented as I? We humans, being so much poorer in our ability to smell and hear than even a lapdog, are left utterly dependent on our one remaining sense. And even that fails us miserably in the dark.

Living in cities, it's easy to ignore this human failing. But living here, where by late September the night begins spreading its dark tentacles, I am learning to peer into the shadows.

In late fall, as our world spins away from the sun and toward the knife edge of winter, the full moon takes up some of the slack. It's a cold silver moon, not the golden moon of summer. When the new moon is below the horizon, the Milky Way is a wide pearly band that through binoculars turns out to be a Seurat painting in starlight.

In winter, I open the window a crack and the yowls of distant coyotes float in with the icy air. Then the late train from New York City, each wheel's clack on the track clear in the still air. The coyotes recede with the train until all seem like sounds from the edge of a dream. A long icicle hangs over half the window. I reach out to it, and it snaps off silently.

The air, windless, smells of frozen moonlight and the silver wash that bathes the world. All sound has been frozen into silence. But they're out there, the hawk and the mice, the coyotes and the red fox, the buds on the apple trees and the bees that will work them. I listen to the silence of all I cannot see.

I try to open my mind to the cosmos, to comprehend the forces, the smallest wisdom, a wisp of revelation in the presence of such grandeur. Then I close the window, cold, earthbound.

"Do *not* get curtains," a friend said as my writing group toured the house. I was pointing at the wall-sized window in the guest room where the spring and summer sun forces guests to rise at a cruel hour.

My friends had, as they kindly put it, "heard a few mentions about too many guests."

"And stop serving pancakes with your home-made maple syrup," concurred another woman in the group.

"And tell them only the outdoor shower works," was the next suggestion. "That should eliminate half the visitors, even in summer."

But definitely "*no curtains*" was the unanimous verdict.

In our bedroom, where we do have curtains, I refuse to close them on any but the most bitter nights. I have a passion for light, and the earlier it arrives, the better.

On summer mornings, I watch the sun conquer the dark in one rapid movement. Instantly, the world pulsates with this early light.

On many mornings we wake to a disappeared world. Suffocatingly low clouds hang heavy over us. They blow up silently from the valley, a sinister curtain, isolating, space both filled and empty. Stepping out, the cloud suffuses my cheeks, wets my lungs, hangs on my lashes, my shoulders. I am a squashed bug.

Then, late in the afternoon, the air suddenly clears in the west, and row upon row of the Adirondack peaks crest, each fired into a rosy mirage by some other sun from some other world. We watch that shimmering pink world while dark clouds continue to churn above.

And so the days and nights roll by, a pageant of big and small displays. I am learning to mark time as the ancients did, by the position of the rising and setting sun, by its low or full arc, by the growth of the moon. We have a calendar on the wall and I have one on my phone, but I guard the privilege of living each day beneath the sky.

ACKNOWLEDGEMENTS

Writing this book was a labor of love, which nevertheless demanded uncommon effort and dedication. The encouragement I received from so many was crucial in keeping me on task for four years.

For their keen intelligence and unstinting encouragement I am grateful to the members of my writing group: Robin Anderson, Victoria Crain, Susan Farrow, Pat Hunter, Janet Warren and Michael Wells.

Yvonne Daley, my editor, freely shared her vast experience and talent, suggesting both cutting and adding, making the revision process both frustrating and fruitful. This book would have been longer and weaker without her months of cheerful reading, rereading and re-rereading. I thank her for devoting so much of her valuable time to this project.

My brilliant daughter, Daniela Molnar, who gave up beach reading to plow through my manuscript, and somehow found the hours needed to apply her talent and training to designing and illustrating the book.

My good friend Jane Linker, who despite her avowed lack of interest in nature writing, was the first to volunteer to read the manuscript and offered invaluable input and encouragement at an early stage.

The superb nature writers whose books and articles provided years of reading pleasure and information, and confirmed that there are others who enjoy this obscure genre.

Last but not least, my husband Ted, who gracefully accepted my need for solitude to think and write.

I am deeply grateful to all.

Sources

Because this is not a scholarly work, I have relied on common knowledge in much of the nature writing, gleaning ideas and background from various sources including the weekly "Environment" and "The Outside Story" columns in the *Rutland Herald,* and from *Northern Woodlands* magazine. For specific information on the life of plants, I consulted my old textbook, *Introduction to Plant Biology* by Kinglsey R. Stern, and *Botany for Gardeners* by Brian Capon. For detailed information about birds I relied on *Silence of the Songbirds* by Bridget Stutchbury and on personal observations in our fields by Roy Pilcher, the Audubon expert in our area. *The Nature of Vermont* by Charles W. Johnson was my go-to source for specifics on the state's geologic, natural and human pasts.

I owe a debt of gratitude to Edward Abbey, Annie Dillard, Verlyn Klinkenborger, Aldo Leopold, Michael Pollan, Ted Levin, Bill McKibben, Janisse Ray, Franklin Russell, and E.O. Wilson whose brilliant works have been a source of inspiration for this book, and for my life.

About the Author

Martha Leb Molnar is a writer, commentator and public relations professional. Her commentaries on Vermont from a newcomer's perspective air regularly on Vermont Public Radio. Her writing has been featured in the anthologies *Peak Experiences: Danger, Death, and Daring in the Mountains of the Northeast*; *Making Connections: Mother-Daughter Travel Adventures*; and *Wild With Child: Adventures of Families in the Great Outdoors*. Earlier in her career, she wrote for *The New York Times* and other newspapers. She earned a certificate in botany from the New York Botanical Gardens and uses what she learned throughout *Taproot: Coming Home to Prairie Hill*, which is her first book. Despite her love of writing, Ms. Leb Molnar is only a foul-weather writer. Good weather in any season finds her outside gardening, biking, hiking, swimming or skiing.

Please visit me online at: MarthaLebMolnar.com or visit my Facebook page at: facebook.com/TaprootVermont

Cover design and interior illustrations by Daniela Molnar
Cover illustration "May Mountain" woodcut c.2012 Sabra Field

9/2014

Made in the USA
San Bernardino, CA
17 September 2014